Sayings of the Spartans

Plutarch

Vigeo Press

Sourced from *Moralia*. Trans. Frank Cole Babbit, 1931.

Vigeo Press Reprint, 2018

ISBN
Paperback 978-1-948648-11-0
Epub 978-1-948648-12-7

Contents

Agasicles[1]

1. When someone expressed surprise to Agasicles, king of the Spartans, because, although he was very fond of reading and lectures, yet he would not admit to his presence Philophanes, a learned man, he said, "I want to be a pupil of those whose son I should like to be as well."

2. In answer to a man who raised the question how anyone could possibly rule in safety without the protection of a bodyguard, he said, "If one rules his subjects as fathers rule their sons."[2]

Agesilaus the Great[3]

1. Agesilaus the Great was once chosen by lot to be master of ceremonies at an evening party, and, when he was asked by the slave who poured the wine how much wine he should serve to each man, Agesilaus said, "If much wine has been provided, as much as each one asks for; but if only a little, then give to all equally."

2. When a malefactor endured tortures without flinching, Agesilaus said, "What an out-and-out villain the man is, devoting his endurance and for-

1 One of the early kings of Sparta.

2 *Cf.* Homer, *Od.* II.47.

3 *Cf.* the note on 190F, *supra*. Many anecdotes about Agesilaus may be found in Polyaenus, *Strategemata*, II.1.

titude to such base and shameful purposes!"

3. When someone praised an orator for his ability in making much of small matters, Agesilaus said that a shoemaker is not a good craftsman who puts big shoes on a small foot.[4]

4. When some said to him, "You have agreed," and kept repeating the same thing, Agesilaus said, "Yes, of course, if it is right; but if not, then I said so, but I did not agree." And when the other added, "But surely kings ought to carry out 'whatsoe'er they confirm by royal assent,'"[5] Agesilaus said, "No more than those who approach kings ought to ask for what is right and say what is right, trying to hit upon the right occasion and a request fitting for kings to grant."

5. Whenever he heard people blaming or praising, he thought it was no less necessary to inform himself about the ways of those who spoke than of those about whom they spoke.[6]

6. When he was still a boy, at a celebration of the festival of the naked boys the director of the dance assigned him to an inconspicuous place; and he obeyed, although he was destined to be king,[7] saying, "Good! I shall show that it is not the places that make men to be held in honour, but the men the places."[8]

---

4 *Cf. Moralia,* 224C, *infra,* and Cicero, *De oratore,* I.54 (231).

5 Adapted from Homer, *Il.* I.527.

6 In almost the same words, but with a different turn of the thought, in Xenophon, *Agesilaus,* 11.4.

7 Plutarch in his *Life of Agesilaus,* chaps. I and II (596A and 597B), says that Agesilaus was brought up as a private citizen, and did not become king until after the death of Agis.

8 *Cf. Moralia,* 149A. In 219, *infra* the remark is attributed to Damonidas, and Diogenes Laertius, II.73, assigns it to Aristippus.

7. When a physician prescribed for him an over-elaborate course of treatment, not at all simple, he said, "Egad, it is not ordained that I must live at all hazards, and I refuse to submit to everything."[9]

8. As he was standing at the altar of Athena of the Brazen House sacrificing a heifer, a louse bit him; but he did not turn a hair, and, picking it off, he cracked it openly before the eyes of all, saying, "By Heaven, it is a pleasure to kill the plotter even at the altar."

9. At another time he saw a mouse being dragged from a hole by a boy who had hold of him, and the mouse turned and bit the hand that held him and escaped; whereupon Agesilaus called the attention of the bystanders to this, and said, "When the smallest animal thus defends itself against those who do it wrong, consider what it becomes men to do."[10]

10. Desiring to bring about the war against the Persian for the sake of setting free the Greeks living in Asia, he consulted the oracle of Zeus at Dodona, and when the god bade him to go on, he reported the answer to the Ephors. And they bade him go to Delphi and ask the same question. Accordingly he proceeded to the prophetic shrine and put his question in this form: "Apollo, are you of the same opinion as your father?" And Apollo concurring, Agesilaus was chosen, and began the campaign.[11]

11. Tissaphernes, at the outset, in fear of Agesilaus, made a treaty, agreeing that the king should leave him the Greek cities free and independent, but, after sending for a great army from the king,

9 *Cf.* the similar attitude of Pompey, 204B, *supra*.

10 *Cf.* the similar story about Brasidas in *Moralia*, 79E, 190B, and 219C.

11 *Cf. Moralia*, 191B, *supra*, and the note.

he declared war on Agesilaus unless he should depart from Asia. Agesilaus gladly welcomed the transgression, and set forth as if he were intending to advance into Caria; and when Tissaphernes had concentrated his forces there, Agesilaus, by a rapid movement thence, invaded Phrygia; and having taken very many cities and a wealth of spoil, he said to his friends, "To do wrong after making a treaty is impious, but to outwit the enemy is not only right and reputable, but also pleasant and profitable."[12]

12. Finding himself inferior in horsemen, he retreated to Ephesus, and there made proclamation to the men of means that they should each provide a horse and a man, and thus gain their own release from service. As a result there were collected, in a very short time, both horses and capable men in place of wealthy cowards.[13] Agesilaus said he was emulating Agamemnon; for Agamemnon accepted a good mare and released from service a base man of wealth.[14]

13. When, in obedience to his orders that the prisoners of war be sold naked, those charged with selling the spoils so offered them, there were many buyers for the clothing, but as for the prisoners' bodies, altogether white and soft because of their indoor life, the buyers derided them as useless and worthless. And Agesilaus, stepping up, said, "These are the things for which you fight, and these are the men whom you fight."[15]

---

12 *Cf.* Plutarch's *Life of Agesilaus,* chap. ix (600C); Xenophon, *Hellenica,* III.4.5 ff., *Agesilaus,* 1.10; Diodorus, XIV.79; Polyaenus, *Strategemata,* II.

13 *Cf.* Plutarch's *Life of Agesilaus,* chap. ix (600D); Xenophon, *Hellenica,* III.4.15, and *Agesilaus,* 1.24.

14 *Cf. Moralia,* 32F. The reference is to Homer, *Il.* XXIII.296 ff.

15 *Cf.* Plutarch's *Life of Agesilaus,* chap. ix (600E); Xenophon, *Helleni-*

14. Having routed Tissaphernes in the Lydian country and slain a great many of his men, he proceeded to overrun the king's country. The king sent money to him, and in return asked for a cessation of hostilities, but Agesilaus said that the State alone had the power to make peace, and that it gave him more pleasure to enrich his soldiers than to be rich himself, and that he thought it a grand thing that the Greeks did not accept gifts from the enemy, but took spoils instead.[16]

15. When Megabates, Spithridates' son, who was most fair of form, came near to him as if to greet him with a kiss because the boy felt that he was held in affection by Agesilaus, Agesilaus drew back. And when the boy stopped coming to see him, Agesilaus asked for him; whereupon his friends said that he had only himself to blame, because he shrank from coming within kissing distance of the fair one, and if he would not act the coward, the boy would come again. Agesilaus, reflecting by himself for no brief time in uninterrupted silence, finally said "There is no need of our trying to persuade him; for I feel that I had rather be above such things than to take by storm the most populous city of our opponents, since it is better to preserve one's own liberty than to deprive others of theirs."[17]

16. In almost all matters he was exact in observing the law, but in anything affecting his friends he thought that too rigid justice in dealings with them was but a poor excuse. At any rate, there is a note of

---

ca, iii.4.19, *Agesilaus*, 1.28; Polyaenus, ii.1.5; Athenaeus, 550e.

16 *Cf.* Plutarch's *Life of Agesilaus*, chap. x (601a-b), where the remark is made to Tithraustes, who was sent by the king to supplant Tissaphernes. *Cf.* also Xenophon, *Hellenica*, iii.4.25, a.

17 *Cf.* Plutarch's *Life of Agesilaus*, chap. xi (602a); *Moralia*, 31c (81a); Xenophon, *Agesilaus*, 5.4-5.

his in circulation addressed to Hidrieus the Carian, in which he asks for the release of one of his friends in this words: "If Nicias is not guilty, let him go; but if he is guilty, let him go for my sake; but let him go anyway."[18]

17. Such, then, was Agesilaus in his friends' behalf in most matters; but there are instances when, in meeting a critical situation, he showed more regard for the general weal. At any rate, on a time when camp was being broken in some disorder, and Agesilaus was leaving behind his loved one who was ill, and the loved one implored him and called him back with tears, Agesilaus, turning round, exclaimed, "How hard it is to be merciful and sensible at the same time!"[19]

18. The mode of living which he followed personally was in no wise better than that of his associates. He refrained always from overeating and from heavy drinking. Sleep he treated, not as a master, but as governed at all times by what he had to do; and such was his attitude towards heat and cold that he alone was able to make good use of the different seasons; and in his tent, which was in the midst of his soldiers, he had no better bed than anybody else.[20]

19. He was continually saying that the commander ought rightly to be superior to the privates not in soft living and luxury, but in endurance and courage.[21]

---

18 *Cf.* Plutarch's *Life of Agesilaus*, chap. xiii (603B); *Moralia*, 191B, *supra*.

19 *Cf.* Plutarch's *Life of Agesilaus*, chap. xiii (603C); *Moralia*, 191A, *supra*.

20 *Cf.* Plutarch's *Life of Agesilaus*, chap. xiv (603D); Xenophon, *Agesilaus*, 5.2-3, and 9.5; Cornelius Nepos, XVII, *Agesilaus*, 5.2.

21 *Cf.* Xenophon, *Agesilaus*, 5.2.

20. At any rate, when someone inquired what advantage the law of Lycurgus had brought to Sparta, he said, "Contempt for pleasures."

21. In answer to the man who expressed surprise at the plainness of the clothes and the fare both of himself and of the other Spartans, he said, "From this mode of life, my friend, we reap a harvest of liberty."

22. When someone else urged him to relax, and said that, because of the uncertainty of fortune, the opportunity for this might never come to him, he replied, "I accustom myself by training to seek to find a change in no change."

23. Even when he had grown old, he followed the same course; and in answer to someone who asked him the reason why, at his age, he went about with no undergarment in such very cold weather, he said, "So that the young men may imitate, having the oldest men and the officials as an example."[22]

24. The Thasians, as he was marching through their country with his army, sent to him flour, geese, sweetmeats, honey-cakes, and other costly foods and drinks of all kinds. The flour alone he accepted, but the rest of the things he bade those who had brought them to carry back because these were of no use to the Spartans. But when the Thasians importuned him and begged him by all means to take all, he gave orders to distribute them among the Helots. And when the Thasians inquired the reason, he said, "It is not in keeping that those who practise manly virtues should indulge in such gormandizing, for things that allure the servile crowd are alien to free men."[23]

---

22 *Cf.* Aelian, *Varia Historia*, vii.13.

23 *Cf.* Plutarch's *Life of Agesilaus*, chap. xxxvi (616f), where the scene

25. At another time the Thasians, because of a feeling that they had been greatly befriended by him, honoured him with temples and deifications, and also sent an embassy to inform him of their action. When he had read the honours which the ambassadors proffered to him, he asked if their country had the power to deify men; and when they answered in the affirmative, he said, "Go to; make gods of yourselves first, and if you can accomplish this, then will I believe that you will be able to make a god of me also."

26. When the Greek peoples of Asia voted to erect statues of him in their most prominent cities, he wrote to them: "Let there be no image of me painted or sculptured or constructed."[24]

27. Seeing in Asia a house roofed with square beams, he asked the owner if timber in that country grew square. And when the man said, "No, but round," he said, "Well, then, if they were square, would you finish them round?"[25]

28. Being asked once how far the bounds of Sparta extended, he said, with a flourish of his spear, "As far as this can reach."[26]

29. When someone else wished to know why Sparta was without walls, he pointed to the citizens in full armour and said, "These are the Spartans'

---

is laid in Egypt, as also in Cornelius Nepos, XVII, *Agesilaus*, 8.3-4. The story is found also in Athenaeus, 657B, and in Aelian, *Varia Historia*, III.20, where it is told of Lysander.

24 *Cf. Moralia*, 191D, *supra*, and the note. By "constructed" he probably refers to the gold and ivory statues which were common among the Greeks.

25 *Cf. Moralia*, 227C, *infra*, and Plutarch's *Life of Lycurgus*, chap. xii (47C).

26 *Cf. Moralia*, 190E (3), *supra*, and 217E (7), 218F (2), 229C (6), *infra*, and 267C.

walls."[27]

30. When another person put the same question, he said, "Cities ought not to be fortified with stones and timbers, but with the strong virtues of their inhabitants."[28]

31. He advised his friends to endeavour to be rich, not in money, but in bravery and virtue.

32. Whenever he wished a task to be quickly performed by his soldiers, he himself took hold first in the sight of all.[29]

33. He found more cause for pride in his working quite as hard as anybody, and in his mastery over himself, rather than in his being king.[30]

34. When he saw a lame Spartan going forth to war and asking where he could get a horse, Agesilaus said, "Don't you realize that war has need, not of those who run away, but of those who stand their ground?"[31]

35. Being asked how he had fostered his great repute, he said, "By showing contempt for death."[32]

36. When someone desired to know why Spartans do battle amidst the sound of fifes, he said, "So that, as all keep step to the music, the cowardly and the brave may be plainly seen."[33]

---

27 *Cf. Moralia*, 217E, *infra* (Antalcidas); Plutarch's *Life of Lycurgus*, chap. xix (52B); Plato, *Laws*, 778D; Epictetus, in Stobaeus, *Florilegium*, v. iii; D.

28 See note *d* on previous page.

29 *Cf.* Xenophon, *Agesilaus*, 5.3. Plutarch tells the same sort of thing about C. Marius in his *Life*, chap. vii (409B).

30 *Cf. Moralia*, 198E (8), *supra*.

31 *Cf.* 217C, 234E, *infra*; Valerius Maximus, III.7, ext. 8.

32 *Cf.* 216C (18), *infra*.

33 *Cf.* Thucydides, v.70; Xenophon, *Constitution of Sparta*, 13.8; Lu-

37. When someone dwelt upon the great good fortune of the king of Persia, who was a very young man, Agesilaus said, "But even Priam at that time of life had not met with misfortune."[34]

38. When he had brought a great part of Asia under his control, he decided to march against the king himself, so that he might put an end to the king's spending his time in leisure and corrupting the popular leaders among the Greeks.[35]

39. When he was summoned home by the Ephors because of the war declared against Sparta by the surrounding Greek states, influenced by the money which had been sent to them by the Persian, he said that the good commander ought to be subject to the command of the laws, and sailed away from Asia, leaving behind a great yearning for him among the Greeks there.[36]

40. Inasmuch as the Persian coinage was stamped with the figure of a bowman, he said, as he was breaking camp, that he was being driven out of Asia by the king with thirty thousand bowmen; for such was the number of gold pieces brought to Athens and Thebes through Timocrates and distributed among the popular leaders; and thus the people were stirred to hostilities against the Spartans.[37]

---

cian, *On Dancing*, 10; Cicero, *Tusculan Disputations*, II.16 (37); Valerius Maximus, II.6.2.

34 *Cf. Moralia*, 113E.

35 *Cf.* Plutarch's *Life of Agesilaus*, chap. xv (603E); Xenophon, *Hellenica*, III.5.1, and IV.1.41, and *Agesilaus*, 1.7.

36 *Cf.* Plutarch's *Life of Agesilaus*, chap. xv (603E); Xenophon, *Hellenica*, IV.2.1-3, and *Agesilaus*, 1.36; Cornelius Nepos, xvii, *Agesilaus*, 4.1-4.

37 *Cf.* Plutarch's *Life of Agesilaus*, chap. xv (604C); *Life of Artaxerxes*, chap. xx (1021D); Xenophon, *Hellenica*, III.5.1. Xenophon *(l.c.)* says that the Persian.

41. He wrote a letter in reply to the Ephors as follows:

> "Agesilaus to the Ephors greeting.
>
> "We hae conquered the maist part of Asia, and made the barbarians rin, an' in Ionia we hae built mony an armed camp. But gin ye bid me come back as ye hae set the limit, I'll come after the letter, or I'll mebbe get there afore it; for I rule, no for masel', but for the State and oor allies. An' a mon truly rules richt whan he gangs wi' the laws an' the Ephors or whatever ither rulers there may be in the State."[38]

42. When he had crossed the Hellespont and was marching through Thrace he made no request of any of the barbarian peoples, but sent to each to inquire whether, as he passed through their country, he should find it friendly or hostile. Nearly all received him in a friendly manner, and helped him on; but the people called Trallians, to whom as it is said even Xerxes gave gifts, demanded of Agesilaus, as the price for passing through their land, an hundred talents of silver and an equal number of women. And he, making fun of them, asked why they did not come at once to get all this, and leading on his forces to where the Trallians were drawn up for battle, he engaged them, and having routed them with great slaughter, he marched through.[39]

43. To the king of the Macedonians he sent to propound the same question; and when the king said that he would consider it, Agesilaus said, "Let him consider it, then, but we will be marching on." Amazed at his boldness, and fearful, the king ac-

38 The letter contains a suspicious number of words for a Laconic letter!.

39 Nos. 42, 43, and 44 are to be found consecutively in nearly the same word in Plutarch's *Life of Agesilaus*, chap. xvi (604D-E).

cordingly bade him advance as a friend.[40]

44. Since the Thessalians were in alliance with his enemies, he ravaged their country. To Larissa, however, he sent Xenocles and Scythes to suggest an amicable agreement. But when these were seized and detained, the rest of his men bore it very ill, and thought that ought to encamp about Larissa and lay siege to it. But he declared that he would not lose either one of those men for the whole of Thessaly, and got them back by coming to terms with the enemy.[41]

45. When he learned that a battle had been fought in the vicinity of Corinth,[42] and that only a very few of the Spartans had fallen, but a vast number of the Corinthians and Athenians and the others on their side, he was not observed to be overjoyful or elated at the victory, but with a very deep sigh said, "Hech, sirs, for Greece, wha her ane sel' had killed sae mony men — as mony as micht pit doon a' the barbarians."[43]

46. When the Pharsalians beset him and harassed his army, he routed them with five hundred horsemen, and set up a trophy at the foot of Mount Narthacium. And he was better satisfied with this victory than with all others, because he himself by his own efforts had built up this company of cavalry,[44] and with this alone he had overcome those

40 Ibid.

41 See note *b* on previous page.

42 In 394 B.C. *Cf.* Xenophon, *Hellenica*, IV.2.18 ff.

43 *Cf.* Plutarch's *Life of Agesilaus*, chap. XV (604F); *Moralia*, 191A (6), *supra*, and the note; Xenophon, *Hellenica*, IV.3.1, *Agesilaus*, 7.4; Diodorus, XIV.867; Cornelius Nepos, XVII, *Agesilaus*, 5.2.

44 See 209B, *supra*.

who took the greatest pride in horsemanship.[45]

47. Diphridas[46] brought word to him from home that he should at once, as he passed by, invade Boeotia. It had been his purpose to do this later after making more adequate preparation, but he did not disobey those in authority, and, after sending for two divisions of the army in the field at Corinth, he entered Boeotia. At Coroneia he engaged in battle Thebans, Athenians, Argives, Corinthians, and the two Locrian peoples, and, although he was in desperate straits by reason of the many wounds in his body, he was victorious in the greatest battle, as Xenophon says,[47] of those fought in his day.[48]

48. After he returned home he made no change in anything touching his life and his manner of living on account of so many successes and victories.[49]

49. Seeing that some of the citizens thought themselves to be somebody and gave themselves great airs because they kept a racing stud, he persuaded his sister Cynisca to enter a chariot in the races at Olympia, for he wished to demonstrate to the Greeks that this sort of thing was no sign of excellence, but only of having money and being willing to spend it.[50]

50. He had with him Xenophon the philosopher,

---

45 *Cf.* Plutarch's *Life of Agesilaus*, chap. xvi (605A); Xenophon, *Hellenica*, IV.3.3-9, *Agesilaus*, 2.2-5.

46 One of the Ephors.

47 *Hellenica*, IV.3.16, *Agesilaus*, 2.9. Xenophon took part in the battle (*Anabasis*, V.3.6).

48 *Cf.* Plutarch's *Life of Agesilaus*, chaps. xvii and xviii (605A-F); Xenophon, *Hellenica*, IV.3.15-20, *Agesilaus*, 2.9-16.

49 *Cf.* Plutarch's *Life of Agesilaus*, chap. xix (606B-C).

50 *Cf.* Plutarch's *Life of Agesilaus*, chap. xx (606D); Xenophon, *Agesilaus*, 9.6; Pausanias, III.8.1-2; III.15.1; V.12.5; VI.1.6; and.

who was treated with marked consideration, and he urged Xenophon to send for his sons, and bring them up in Sparta, where they would be taught the fairest of all lessons — to rule and to be ruled.[51]

51. On one other occasion he was asked what was the especial reason why the Spartans were fortunate above all other peoples, and he replied, "Because they, above all others, make it their practice to rule and to be ruled."[52]

52. After Lysander's death he found a huge association banded together, which Lysander, immediately after his return from Asia, had organized against him, and he set out to show up Lysander by pointing out what kind of a citizen he had been when he was alive. So, after reading a speech which had been left among Lysander's papers, the author of which was Cleon of Halicarnassus, and which Lysander had been intending to appropriate and deliver before the people on the subject of revolution and changing the form of government, Agesilaus wished to make it public. But when one of the aged men read the speech, and was frightened at its cleverness, and advised him not to disinter the dead Lysander, but rather to inter the speech along with him, he took the advice and did nothing.[53]

53. Those who covertly opposed him he did not openly put to confusion, but managed to have some of them always sent out as generals and officers, and then he would proceed to demonstrate that they had proved themselves unprincipled and

51 *Cf.* Plutarch's *Life of Agesilaus*, chap. xx (606D), and Diogenes Laertius, II.51 and 54.

52 *Cf. Moralia*, 215C, *infra*; Plutarch's *Life of Lycurgus*, chap. xxx (58C), and *Life of Agesilaus*, chap. i (596D); Xenophon, *Agesilaus*, 2.16.

53 *Cf. Moralia*, 229F, *infra*; Plutarch's *Life of Lysander*, chap. xxiv (447D), and chap. xxx (450E); *Life of Agesilaus*, chap. xx (606E).

greedy in exercising their authority. Then later, when they were brought to trial, his rôle this time would be to help them and defend them at their trial; and thus he won their allegiance, and brought them over to his own side, so that there was nobody who opposed him.[54]

54. Somebody wanted him to write to his friends in Asia so that the petitioner might meet with right treatment there. "But," said Agesilaus, "my friends of themselves do what is right, even if I do not write to them."

55. Somebody in a foreign land pointed out to Agesilaus the city wall, high towering and exceedingly massive in its construction, and asked Agesilaus if it looked grand to him. "Yes," said Agesilaus, "grand indeed, not for men though, but for women to live in."[55]

56. When a man from Megara boasted greatly about his city, Agesilaus said, "Young man, your words need a great power to back them."[56]

57. Things which he saw other people admiring he seemed not even to notice. For example, once upon a time Callippides, the tragic actor,[57] who had a name and repute among the Greeks, and was received everywhere with the most flattering attention, first of all put himself in front of Agesilaus

---

54 *Cf.* Plutarch's *Life of Agesilaus*, chap. xx (606F).

55 *Cf. Moralia*, 190A, *supra*, 215D, 230C, *infra*, and Valerius Maximus, III.7, ext. 8.

56 The remark is usually attributed to Lysander; *cf.* Plutarch's *Life of Lysander*, chap. xxii (445D); *Moralia* 71E, 190E, *supra*, 229C, *infra*; Themistius, *Oration* xxvii. 334C. The idea was originally expressed by Adeimantus to Themistocles in Herodotus, VIII.61.

57 Famous for his impressive acting. *Cf.* Xenophon, *Symposium*, 3.11; Aristotle, *Poetics*, chap. 26; Plutarch, *Moralia*, 348E; Polyaenus, *Strategemata*, VI.10.

and addressed him, and then pompously thrust himself into the company that was walking with him, thus making it plain that he expected the king to begin some friendly conversation, and finally he said, "Your Majesty, do you not recognize me, and have you not heard who I am?" At that Agesilaus looked towards him and said, "Are ye no Callippidas the shawman?" That is what the Spartans call the strolling players.[58]

58. When he was invited to hear the man who imitated the nightingale's voice, he begged to be excused, saying, "I hae heard the bird itsel' mony a time."[59]

59. Menecrates the physician, who, because of his success in curing certain persons who had been given up to die, had come to be called Zeus, used to drag in this title on all occasions, and even went so far in his effrontery as to write to Agesilaus in this fashion: "Menecrates Zeus to King Agesilaus, health and happiness." Agesilaus did not read any further, but wrote in reply, "King Agesilaus to Menecrates, health and sanity!"[60]

60. When Conon and Pharnabazus with the Great King's fleet were masters of the sea and blockaded the Spartans' coast, and the walls of Athens had been rebuilt[61] with the money provided by Pharnabazus, the Spartans made peace with the

58 *Cf.* Plutarch's *Life of Agesilaus,* chap. xxi (607D).

59 *Life of Agesilaus,* chap. xxi (607E); *Moralia,* 191B; *Life of Lycurgus,* chap. xx (52E). A similar remark is attributed to Pleistarchus, *Moralia,* 231C.

60 *Cf. Moralia,* 191A (5), *supra,* and Plutarch's *Life of Agesilaus,* chap. xxi (607E). Ascribed to Philip of Macedon by Aelian, *Varia Historia,* XII.51, and Athena.

61 In 393 B.C. (Xenophon, *Hellenica,* IV.8.10).

king.[62] They sent one of their citizens, Antalcidas, to Tiribazus, and surrendered into the king's power those Greeks in Asia Minor for whose freedom Agesilaus had fought. It follows, therefore, that Agesilaus could not have had the slightest thing to do with this disreputable business; for Antalcidas was at enmity with him, and employed every resource in working for the peace, because he felt that the war made Agesilaus great and enhanced his repute and importance.[63]

61. Yet, in answer to a man who said that the Spartans were becoming pro-Persian, Agesilaus said that rather the Persians were becoming pro-Spartan![64]

62. Being asked once which was better of the virtues, bravery or justice, he said that there is no use for bravery unless justice is also in evidence, and if all men should become just they would have no need of bravery.[65]

63. The inhabitants of Asia were accustomed to give to the king of Persia the title of 'The Great,' but Agesilaus said, "In what, pray, is he greater than I, unless he is more just and more self-controlled?"[66]

64. He used to say that the inhabitants of Asia were poor freemen, but good slaves.[67]

65. Being asked how one might most surely

---

62 The peace of Antalcidas, 387 B.C. (Xenophon, *Hellenica,* v.1.29; Plutarch, *Life of Artaxerxes,* chap. xxi (1022A)).

63 *Cf.* Plutarch's *Life of Agesilaus,* chap. xxiii (608C).

64 *Ibid.* 608D; *cf.* also Plutarch's *Life of Artaxerxes,* chap. xxi (1022C).

65 *Cf. Moralia,* 190F (3), *supra,* and Plutarch's *Life of Agesilaus,* chap. xxiii (608F).

66 *Cf.* the note on *Moralia,* 190F (2), *supra.*

67 *Cf.* the note on *Moralia,* 190F (1), *supra.*

have a good name among men, he said, "If one say what is best and do what is most honourable."

66. He used to say that a general ought to be possessed of boldness towards the enemy and kindness towards the men under him.[68]

67. When someone desired to know what boys ought to learn, he said, "That which they will use when they become men."[69]

68. Once when he was sitting as judge the accuser spoke well and the defendant poorly, merely repeating in answer to each point, "Agesilaus, a king must uphold the laws;" whereat Agesilaus said, "And if somebody had broken into your house, and if somebody had robbed you of your coat, should you expect that the builder of the house or the maker of the coat would come to your assistance?"

69. After the peace was made,[70] a letter from the king of Persia was brought to him, of which the Persian with Callias the Spartan was the bearer, in regard to hospitality and friendship; but Agesilaus would not receive it, bidding the man to take back word to the king that there was no need to send letters to him personally; that if the king showed himself to be a friend to Sparta and well disposed towards Greece, he himself, to the very best of his power, would be a friend to the king. But if the king should be caught plotting against Greece, he went on to say, "even if I receive many letters, let him not believe that he shall have me for a friend."[71]

---

68 Stobaeus, *Florilegium*, LIV.49, adds, "and reasoning power to meet crises.".

69 Leotychidas (224D, *infra*) and Aristippus (Diogenes Laertius, II.80) expressed the same opinion, which has been repeated *ad nauseam* by professors of paedagogy.

70 The peace of Antalcidas, 387 B.C. See *Moralia*, 213A-B, *supra*.

71 *Cf.* Plutarch's *Life of Agesilaus*, chap. xxiii (608F); Xenophon, *Agesi-*

70. He was unusually fond of children, and it is said that at home he used to mount astride a stick as a hobby-horse and play with his children when they were little. But when he was seen thus by one of his friends, he begged the man to tell nobody before he had children of his own.[72]

71. He made war continually upon the Thebans, and when he was wounded in the battle,[73] they say that Antalcidas exclaimed, "This is a fine reward which you are receiving from the Thebans for giving them lessons in fighting when they had no desire to fight, and no knowledge even of fighting!" For, as a fact, they say that the Thebans at that time were more warlike than they had ever been before, owing to the many campaigns of the Spartans against them.[74] It was for this reason that Lycurgus of old, in his so-called 'Decrees,' forbade campaigning frequently against the same peoples, so that these should not learn to make war.[75]

72. When he heard once that the allies had come to be disaffected because of the continual campaigning (for they in great numbers followed the Spartans who were but few), wishing to bring their numbers to the proof, he gave orders that the allies all sit down together indiscriminately and the Spartans separately by themselves; and then, through

---

laus, 8.3 (in almost the same words as here); Aelian, *Varia Historia*, x.20.

72 *Cf.* Plutarch's *Life of Agesilaus*, chap. xxv (610c); Aelian, *Varia Historia*, xii.15. Diogenes Laertius and Valerius Maximus (viii.8, ext. 1), tell this story of Socrates.

73 In the invasion of Boeotia in 378 b.c..

74 *Cf.* Plutarch's *Life of Agesilaus*, chap. xxvi (610d); *Life of Pelopidas*, chap. xv (285d); *Moralia*, 227c, *infra*.

75 *Cf.* Plutarch's *Life of Lycurgus*, chap. xiii (47d), *Moralia*, 189f, *supra*; Polyaenus, *Strategemata*, i.16.2.

the herald, he commanded the potters to stand up first; and when these had done so, he commanded the smiths to stand up next, and then the carpenters in turn, and the builders, and each of the other trades. As a result, pretty nearly all of the allies stood up, but of the Spartans not a single one; for there was a prohibition against their practising or learning any menial calling. And so Agesilaus, with a laugh, said, "You see, men, how many more soldiers we send out than you do."[76]

73. In the battle of Leuctra many Spartans ran away to escape the enemy, and these were liable to disgrace as provided by the law. The Ephors, seeing the State bereft of men when it was in great need of soldiers, wished to do away with the disgrace, and also to observe the laws. Accordingly they chose Agesilaus as lawgiver; and he, coming into the public meeting, said, "I would not become a lawgiver to enact another set of laws, for in the present laws I would make no addition, subtraction, or revision. It is good that our present laws be in full force, beginning with the morrow."[77]

74. Although Epameinondas came on with such an overwhelming tide,[78] and the Thebans and their allies were boasting mightily over the victory, nevertheless Agesilaus kept him out of the city and made him turn back, although the number of persons in the city was very small.[79]

---

76 *Cf.* Plutarch's *Life of Agesilaus*, chap. xxvi (610E); Polyaenus, *Strategemata*, II.1.7.

77 *Cf.* Plutarch's *Life of Agesilaus*, chap. xxx (612F); and the note on *Moralia*, 191C (10), *supra*.

78 The expression is that of Theopompus, as Plutarch tells us in his *Life of Agesilaus*, chap. xxxi (613B).

79 *Cf.* Xenophon, *Hellenica*, VII.5.10; Diodorus, XV.83; Cornelius Nepos, XVII, *Agesilaus*, 6.1-3.

75. In the battle of Mantineia he urged the Spartans to pay no attention to any of the others, but to fight against Epameinondas, for he said that only men of intelligence are valiant and may be counted upon to bring victory; if, therefore, they could make away with that one man, they would very easily reduce the others to subjection; for these were unintelligent and worthless. And so it came to pass. For while the victory rested with Epameinondas, and the rout of the enemy was complete, as he turned and was cheering on his men, one of the Spartans struck him a fatal blow; and when he had fallen, Agesilaus's men, rallying from their flight, made the victory hang in the balance, and the Thebans showed themselves far inferior, and the Spartans far superior.

76. When Sparta was in need of money for war, and was supporting a mercenary force, Agesilaus set out for Egypt, having been summoned by the king of the Egyptians for a goodly remuneration. But because of the simplicity of his clothes he came into contempt among the people there; for they had been expecting that they should see the king of Sparta, like the king of Persia, with his person magnificently apparelled — a sorry opinion for them to hold regarding kings. At any rate, he showed them, before they were done with him, that the proper way to acquire greatness and distinction is by understanding and manly virtues.[80]

77. When he saw that his men were on the point of capitulating, for fear of the oncoming danger because of the vast number of the enemy (two hundred thousand) and the small number with him, he determined, before drawing up the battle-line,

80 *Cf.* Plutarch's *Life of Agesilaus*, chap. xxxvi (616B); Cornelius Nepos, xvii, *Agesilaus*, 7.2.

to forestall this by a plan unknown to the others. And upon his hand he wrote the word victory with the letters turned toward the left. Then, as he received the liver from the priest, he placed it on the hand which had the writing upon it. Holding it for rather a long time, he showed perplexity, and kept up a pretence of not knowing what to do, until the marks of the letters had been taken up by the liver and imprinted upon it. Then he exhibited it to those who with him were to engage in the struggle, saying that the gods through the letters had revealed victory. So his men, feeling that they had a sure sign that they were to overcome the enemy, became bold for the battle.[81]

78. While the enemy were digging a ditch to surround his position (as they could do by reason of their vast numbers), and Nectanabis, with whom he was allied, was insistent upon a sortie and a decisive battle, Agesilaus said that he would not hinder the enemy in their desire to put themselves on equal terms with the defenders. And when the trench lacked but little of completion, he drew up his men in the open space between the ends, and, fighting with equal numbers against equal numbers, he routed the enemy with great slaughter by means of few soldiers with him, and sent home much money for the State.[82]

79. On his way home from Egypt death came to him, and in his last hours he gave directions to those with him that they should not cause to be made any sculptured or painted or imitative representation of his person. "For if I have done any

81 A similar trick of Alexander's is told by Frontinus, *Strategemata*, I.11.14.

82 *Cf.* Plutarch's *Life of Agesilaus*, chap. xxxix (618A), *Moralia*, 191C (11), *supra*, and the note.

goodly deed, that shall be my memorial; but if not, then not all the statues in the world, the works of menial and worthless men, will avail."[83]

Agesipolis, son of Cleombrotus[84]

1. Agesipolis, son of Cleombrotus, when somebody said that Philip in a few days had razed Olynthus to the ground, said, "By Heaven, he will not build another like it in many years!"[85]

2. When someone else remarked that he while king had been made hostage with those in the prime of life, and not their children or their women, he said, "That is but just, for it is good that we ourselves should bear the consequences of our own mistakes."

3. When he wished to send for some dogs from home, and some said, "There is no such export permitted from there," he said, "Nor was there of men before this; but now it has been done!"

Agesipolis, son of Pausanias[86]

Agesipolis, the son of Pausanias, when the Athenians offered to accept the city of Megara as arbitrator regarding some complaints which they had each against the other, said, "It is a shame, men of Athens, that those who have held the hegemony of the Greeks should know less about justice than

83 *Cf. Moralia,* 191D (12), *supra,* and the note.

84 Agesipolis II, king of Sparta, 371-370 B.C..

85 *Cf. Moralia,* 40E and 458B.

86 King of Sparta, 394-380 B.C..

the Megarians."

AGIS, SON OF ARCHIDAMUS[87]

1. Once upon a time the Ephors said to Agis the son of Archidamus, "Take the young men and march against the country of this man here. He will himself guide you to its citadel." "And how, sirs," said Agis, "is it right to entrust so many youths to a man who is betraying his own country?"[88]

2. Being asked what form of instruction was most in vogue in Sparta, he said, "Knowledge of how to rule and to be ruled."[89]

3. He said that the Spartans did not ask 'how many are the enemy,' but 'where are they?'[90]

4. When, at Mantineia, he was not permitted to risk a decisive battle with the enemy, who outnumbered his men, he said, "He who would rule over many must fight with many."[91]

5. When someone inquired how many Spartans there were, he said, "Enough to keep all bad men away."[92]

6. As he was going about among the walls of the Corinthians and observed that they were high and towering and vast in extent, he said, "What women

87 Agis II, king of Sparta, 427-401 B.C. Some of the sayings attributed to him here should doubtless be assigned to the younger Agis (Agis III).

88 See the note on *Moralia*, 191E (2), *supra*, where the saying is attributed to the younger Agis.

89 *Cf.* the note on 212C (51), *supra*.

90 *Cf.* the note on 190C (1), *supra*.

91 *Cf.* the note on 190C (2), *supra*.

92 *Cf.* the note on 190D (5), *supra*.

live in that place?"[93]

7. When a lecturer said, "Speech is the most important thing of all," he retorted, "Then if you are silent, you are of no worth at all!"

8. When the Argives, after their defeat, met him again with greater boldness, and he saw that his allies were greatly perturbed, he said, "Do not be afraid, men; for when we who are victorious are frightened, what do you think those vanquished by us are doing?"

9. In answer to the ambassador from Abdera, who, after winding up a long discourse, asked him what report he should make to his people at home, he said, "Report that during all the time you wanted to speak I listened in silence."[94]

10. When some commended the people of Elis because they were very just in conducting the Olympic games, he said, "What great or marvellous accomplishment is it if they practise justice on one day only in four years?"[95]

11. In answer to those who said that some members of the other royal house[96] were jealous of him he said, "So then, their own ill fortune will make them miserable and, besides that, the good fortune of myself and of my friends."

12. When someone proffered the advice that they ought to give a passage-way to those of the enemy who were fleeing,[97] he said, "And how, if we do not fight those who because of cowardice are

93 *Cf.* the note on 190A, *supra.*

94 *Cf. Moralia,* 232E (2), *infra.*

95 *Cf.* the note on 190C (3), *supra.*

96 The Spartans had two kings and consequently two royal families.

97 This was a part of the tactics of Agesilaus according to Polyaenus, *Strategemata,* II.1.4. *Cf.* Xenophon, *Hellenica,* IV.2.22 and IV.3.19.

fleeing, shall we fight those who because of bravery stand their ground?"

13. When someone brought forward a plan, for the freedom of the Greeks, which, while not lacking idealism, was difficult to put into practice, he said, "Your words, my friend, need the backing of power and money."[98]

14. When someone said that Philip would make Greece forbidden ground to them, he said, "It is quite enough, my friend, for us to go and come within the confines of our own land."[99]

15. An ambassador who had come from Perinthus to Sparta made a long harangue; and when he had stopped speaking and asked Agis what report he should make to the people of Perinthus, Agis said, "What else except that it was hard for you to stop speaking, and that I said nothing?"[100]

16. He came alone on an embassy to Philip, and when Philip exclaimed, "What is this? Have you come all alone?", he said, "Yes, for I came to only one man."[101]

17. When one of the elderly men said to him in his old age, inasmuch as he saw the good old customs falling into desuetude, and other mischievous practices creeping in, that for this reason everything was getting to be topsy-turvy in Sparta, Agis said humorously, "Things are then but following a logical course if that is what is happening; for when I was a boy, I used to hear from my father that ev-

98 The same idea which is expressed in *Moralia*, 212E (56), *supra*.

99 This remark must have been made by the younger Agis (Agis III).

100 *Cf. Moralia*, 232E (2), *infra*.

101 This remark also must be assigned to the younger Agis. *Cf. Moralia*, 233F (29), *infra*, and 511A, where an unnamed Spartan makes this retort to Demetrius.

erything was topsy-turvy among them; and my father said that, when he was a boy, his father had said this to him; so nobody ought to be surprised if conditions later are worse than those earlier, but rather to wonder if they grow better or remain approximately the same."[102]

18. Being asked how one could be a free man all his life, he said, "By feeling contempt for death."[103]

The Younger Agis[104]

1. The younger Agis, when Demades said that the jugglers who swallow swords use the Spartan swords because of their shortness, retorted, "But all the same the Spartans reach their enemies with their swords."[105]

2. In answer to a base man who asked repeatedly who was the best Spartan, he said, "The one most unlike you."[106]

The Last Agis[107]

Agis, the last of the kings of Sparta, was arrested as the result of treachery and condemned by the Ephors without a trial. As he was being led away to the halter he saw one of the officers weeping, and said, "Stop your weeping for me, man. For in spite

102 The latter part of this has been suspected on account of the length. For the sentiment *cf.* Homer, *Od.* 276-277; Hor. *Odes*, III.6.46; Aratus, *Phaenomena*, 123-127.

103 *Cf. Moralia*, 210F (35), *supra*.

104 Agis III, king of Sparta, 338-331 B.C..

105 *Cf.* the note on 191E (1).

106 *Cf.* the note on 190D (4).

107 Agis IV, king of Sparta, 245-241 B.C..

of my being put to death in such defiance of law and justice, I am superior to those who are taking my life." With these words he willingly offered his neck for the noose.[108]

ACROTATUS[109]

Acrotatus, when his parents claimed it was his duty to co-operate with them in some unjust action, spoke in opposition up to a certain limit. But when they insisted, he said, "While I was with you, I had not the slightest idea of justice; but since you have surrendered me to our country and its laws, and, besides, have had me instructed in justice and honourable conduct so far as lay in your power, I shall try to follow these rather than you. And since your wish is for me to do what is best, and since what is just is best both for a private citizen, and much more so for a ruler, I will do what you wish; but as for what you propose I shall beg to be excused."[110]

ALCAMENES, SON OF TELECLUS[111]

1. Alcamenes, the son of Teleclus, when somebody inquired how a man could best keep a kingdom secure, said, "If he should not hold his own advantage too high."

2. When another person sought to know the reason why he did not accept gifts from the Messenians, he said, "Because if I took gifts, it would be

---

108 *Cf.* Plutarch's *Life of Agis*, chaps. xix-xx (p. 803c).

109 Son of Cleomenes II. He died before his father, and so never became king.

110 *Cf.* a similar remark of Agesilaus, *Moralia*, 534D.

111 King of Sparta, 779-742 B.C. (the date is uncertain).

impossible to maintain peace with impartial regard for the laws."

3. When someone said that he lived a straitened life while possessed of plenty of property, he said, "Yes, for it is a noble thing for one who possesses much to live according to reason and not according to his desires."

Anaxandridas[112]

1. Anaxandridas, the son of Leo, in answer to a man who took much to heart the sentence imposed upon him of exile from the country, said, "My good sir, be not downcast at being an exile from your country but at being an exile from justice."

2. To a man who told the Ephors of things that were needful, but spoke at greater length than would have sufficed, he said, "My friend, in needless time you dwell upon the need!"[113]

3. When someone inquired why they put their fields in the hands of the Helots, and did not take care of them themselves, he said, "It was by not taking care of the fields, but of ourselves, that we acquired those fields."

4. When someone else said that high repute works injury to men and that he who is freed from this will be happy, he retorted, "Then those who commit crimes would, according to your reasoning, be happy. For how could any man, in committing sacrilege or any other crime, be concerned over high repute?"

5. When another person asked why the Spartans, in their wars, ventured boldly into danger, he

112 King of Sparta, *circa* 560-520 B.C..

113 Attributed to Leo, the father of Anaxandridas, in *Moralia*, 224F (3), and to Leonidas, the son of Anaxandridas, in Plutarch's *Life of Lycurgus*, chap. xx (52B).

said, "Because we train ourselves to have regard for life and not, like others, to be timid about it."

6. When someone asked him why the elders continue the trials of capital cases over several days, and why, even if the defendant is acquitted, he is none the less still under indictment, he said, "They take many days to decide, because, if they make an error in a capital case, there can be no reversal of the judgement; and the accused continues, perforce, to be under indictment of the law, because, under this law, it may be possible, by deliberation, to arrive at a better decision."[114]

ANAXANDER, SON OF EURYCRATES[115]

Anaxander, the son of Eurycrates, when someone inquired why the Spartans did not amass money in the public treasury, said, "So that those made the guardians of it may not become corrupt."

ANAXILAS[116]

Anaxilas, in answer to the man who wondered why the Ephors did not rise and offer their places to the kings,[117] and this, too, although they were appointed to their position by the kings, said, "For the very same reason that they hold the office of Ephor."

114 For the fact *cf.* Plato, *Apology*, chap. xxvii (37A); Thucydides, I.132.

115 King of Sparta in the earlier part of the seventh century B.C..

116 Son of Archidamus, perhaps one of the arbiters between Athens and Megara over Salamis, seventh century B.C..

117 *Cf.* Xenophon, *Constitution of Sparta*, 15.6; and Nicolaus quoted by Stobaeus, *Florilegium*, XLIV.41 ad fin..

ANDROCLEIDAS[118]

Androcleidas the Spartan, who had a crippled leg, enrolled himself among the fighting-men. And when some persons were insistent that he be not accepted because he was crippled, he said, "But I do not have to run away, but to stay where I am when I fight the opposing foe."[119]

ANTALCIDAS[120]

1. When Androcleidas was being initiated into the mysteries at Samothrace, he was asked by the priest what especially dreadful thing he had done during his life, and he replied, "If any such deed has been committed by me, the gods themselves will know it."[121]

2. In answer to the Athenian who called the Spartans unlearned, he said, "At any rate we are the only people who have learned no evil from you."[122]

3. When another Athenian said to him, "You must admit that we have many a time put you to rout from the Cephisus," he retorted, "But we have never put you to rout from the Eurotas."[123]

4. Being asked how anybody could best make himself agreeable to the people, he said, "If his conversation with them is most pleasant and his sug-

118 Possibly the opponent of Lysander, mentioned in Plutarch's *Life of Lysander*, chap. viii (437c).

119 *Cf.* the note on *Moralia*, 210F (34), *supra*.

120 See the note on *Moralia*, 192B, *supra*.

121 The same story is told of Lysander in *Moralia*, 229D (1), *infra*, and of an unknown Spartan in *Moralia*, 236D (68), *infra*.

122 *Cf.* the note on *Moralia*, 192B (1), *supra*.

123 *Cf.* the note on *Moralia*, 192C (2), *supra*.

gestions most profitable."[124]

5. When a lecturer was about to read a laudatory essay on Heracles, he said, "Why, who says anything against him?"[125]

6. When Agesilaus was wounded in battle by the Thebans, Androcleidas said to his face, "You have your just reward for the lessons in fighting you have given to that people who had no desire to fight and no knowledge even of fighting." For it appeared that they had been made warlike by the continual campaigns of Agesilaus against them.[126]

7. He used to say that the young men were the walls of Sparta, and the points of their spears its boundaries.[127]

8. In answer to the man who sought to know why the Spartans use short daggers in war, he said, "Because we fight close to the enemy."[128]

ANTIOCHUS

Antiochus, when he was Ephor, hearing that Philip had given Messenians their land, asked if he had also provided them with the power to prevail in fighting to keep it.[129]

AREUS[130]

1. Areus, when some men commended, not

124 *Cf. Moralia,* 213C (65), *supra.*

125 *Cf.* the note on *Moralia,* 192C (3), *supra.*

126 *Cf.* the note on *Moralia,* 189F (5), *supra.*

127 *Cf.* the notes on *Moralia,* 210E (28, 29, 30), *supra.*

128 *Cf.* the note on *Moralia,* 191E, *supra.*

129 Repeated in *Moralia,* 192B, *supra.*

130 Areus I, king of Sparta, 309-265 B.C..

their own wives, but certain wives of other men, said, "By Heaven, there ought to be no random talk about fair and noble women, and their characters ought to be totally unknown save only to their consorts."[131]

2. Once upon a time, when he was passing though Selinus in Sicily, he saw inscribed upon a monument this elegiac couplet:

> these men, who tyranny strove to extinguish,
> Brazen-clad Ares laid low; nigh to our gates
> were they slain.

Whereupon he said, "You certainly deserved to die for trying to extinguish tyranny when it was ablaze; rather you ought to have let it burn itself out completely."[132]

Ariston[133]

1. When someone commended the maxim of Cleomenes, who, on being asked what a good king ought to do, said, "To do good to his friends and evil to his enemies," Ariston said, "How much better, my good sir, to do good to our friends, and to make friends of our enemies?" This, which is universally conceded to be one of Socrates' maxims,[134] is also referred to Ariston.[135]

2. When someone inquired how many Spartans

---

131 *Cf. Moralia*, 220D and 242E, *infra;* Thucydides, II.45.

132 *Cf.* Plutarch's *Life of Lycurgus*, chap. xx (52E).

133 King of Sparta, *circa* 560-510 B.C..

134 But not quite in these words *cf.* Plato, *Republic*, I chap. ix (335B ff.), *Crito*, chap. x (49A ff.), *Gorgias*, 469A-B and 475B-D.

135 A similar remark is attributed to Cleobulus by Diogenes Laertius, I.91.

there were in all, he said, "Enough to keep away our enemies."[136]

3. When one of the Athenians read a memorial oration in praise of those who fell at the hands of the Spartans, he said, "What kind of men, then, do you think ours must be who vanquished these?"[137]

ARCHIDAMIDAS

1. Archidamidas, in answer to a man who commended Charillus because he was gentle towards all alike, said, "And how could any man be justly commended if he be gentle towards the wicked?"[138]

2. When somebody found fault with Hecataeus the sophist because, when he was received as a member at the common table, he spoke not a word, Archidamidas said, "You do not seem to realize that he who knows how to speak knows also the right time for speaking."[139]

ARCHIDAMUS, SON OF ZEUXIDAMUS[140]

1. Archidamus, the son of Zeuxidamus, when someone inquired of him who were at the head of Sparta, said, "The laws and the magistrates in accordance with the laws."

2. In answer to a man who praised a harper and expressed amazement at his ability, he said,

136 *Cf.* the note on *Moralia*, 190D (5), *supra*.

137 Perhaps the remark of another man named Ariston who lived later.

138 *Cf. Moralia*, 55E and 537D.

139 *Cf.* Plutarch's *Life of Lycurgus*, chap. xx (52C).

140 Archidamus II, king of Sparta, 469-427 B.C..

"My good sir, what honours shall you be able to offer to good men when you have such praise for a harper?"

3. When someone, in introducing a musician to him, remarked, "This man is a good musician," he said, "And in this country of ours that man there rates as a good soup-maker," thus implying that there was no distinction between giving pleasure through the sound of instruments and giving it through the preparation of appetizing foods and soup.[141]

4. When somebody promised him to make the wine pleasant to the taste, he said, "What for? For more of it will be used, and it will make the men's eating together less beneficial."[142]

5. As he was establishing his camp hard by the city of Corinth, he saw hares start up from a spot near the wall. He said therefore to his fellow-soldiers, "The enemy are ours."[143]

6. When two persons accepted him as arbiter, he took them to the sacred precinct of Athena of the Brazen House, and made them swear to abide by his decision; and when they had given their oaths, he said, "My decision, then, is that you are not to leave this sacred precinct before you compose your differences."

7. When Dionysius, the despot of Sicily, sent costly raiment to Archidamus' daughters, he would not accept it, saying, "I am afraid that, if the girls

141 *Cf. Moralia*, 223F, *infra* (15), where the saying is attributed to Cleomenes.

142 See *Moralia*, 240D (2), *infra*, which makes the meaning of this passage quite clear.

143 A similar remark is attributed to Lysander in *Moralia*, 190E, *supra*, and 229D, *infra*.

should put it on, they would appear ugly to me."[144]

8. Observing that his son was fighting impetuously against the Athenians, he said, "Either add to your strength, or subtract from your courage."

ARCHIDAMUS, SON OF AGESILAUS[145]

1. Archidamus, the son of Agesilaus, when Philip, after the battle of Chaeroneia, wrote him a somewhat haughty letter, wrote in reply, "If you should measure your own shadow, you would not find that it has become any greater than before you were victorious."

2. Being asked how much land the Spartans controlled, he said, "As much as they can reach with the spear."[146]

3. Periander, the physician, was distinguished in his profession and commended very highly, but was a writer of wretched verses. "Why in the world, Periander," said Archidamus, "do you yearn to be called a bad poet instead of a skilful physician?"

4. In the war against Philip, when some proffered the advice that they ought to engage him in battle at a good distance from their own land,[147] Archidamus said, "No, there is not what we ought to look to, but where, in fighting, we shall be superior to the enemy."

5. In answer to those who commended him when he had been victorious in battle[148] against the

144 *Cf.* the note on *Moralia*, 190D (1), *supra*.

145 Archidamus III, king of Sparta, 361-338 B.C..

146 *Cf.* the note on *Moralia*, 210E (28), *supra*.

147 The policy of Demosthenes (*e.g. Olynthiac* i. *ad fin.*).

148 The "tearless battle" in 368 B.C. described by Xenophon, *Hellenica*,

Arcadians, he said, "It would have been better if he had vanquished them by intelligence rather than by strength."

6. When he invaded Arcadia, he learned that the Eleans were supporting the Arcadians, and so he sent this letter to them: "Archidamus to the Eleans. Quiet is a good thing."[149]

7. In the plebeian war, when his allies sought to know how much money would be sufficient, and said it was only fair that he set a limit to their contributions, he said, "War does not feed on fixed rations."[150]

8. When he saw the missile shot by a catapult, which had been brought then for the first time from Sicily, he exclaimed, "Great Heavens! man's valour is no more!"[151]

9. When the Greeks were not willing to take his advice and break their agreements with Antipater[152] and Craterus the Macedonian, and be free, because of a feeling that the Spartans would be harsher than the Macedonians, he said, "A sheep or a goat bleats always in the same way, but a man talks in a great variety of ways until he accomplishes what he has set his mind upon."

Astycratidas

When someone said to Astycratidas, after the

---

vii.1.28-32. *Cf.* Plutarch's *Life of Agesilaus*, chap. xxxiii (614e).

149 The saying is attributed to Periander by Diogenes Laertius, i.97.

150 *Cf.* the note on *Moralia*, 190a, *supra*. The saying plainly belongs to Archidamus II (218c, *supra*), who lived at the time of the Peloponnesian war. See Plutarch's *Life of Cleomenes*, chap. xxvii (817e).

151 *Cf. Moralia*, 191d, *supra*.

152 Either Antipater (Wyttenbach's certain emendation) or Antigonus (mss.) is too late for Archidamus III, who died in 338 b.c..

defeat of Agis their king in the battle against Antipater in the vicinity of Megalopolis, "What will you do, men of Sparta? Will you be subject to the Macedonians?" he said, "What! Is there any way in which Antipater can forbid us to die fighting for Sparta?"

BIAS[153]

Bias, caught in an ambush by Iphicrates the Athenian general, and asked by his soldiers what was to be done, said, "What else except for you to save your lives and for me to die fighting?"

BRASIDAS[154]

1. Brasidas caught a mouse among some figs, and, when he got bitten, let it go. Then, turning to those who were present, he said, "There is nothing so small that it does not save its life if it has the courage to defend itself against those who would lay hand on it."[155]

2. In a battle he was wounded by a spear which pierced his shield, and, pulling the weapon out of the wound, with this very spear he slew the foe. Asked how he got his wound, he said, "'Twas when my shield turned traitor."[156]

3. As he was going forth to war he wrote to the Ephors, "What I wull to dae I'll dae as regairds the war or be a deid mon."

---

153 It seems almost certain that this anecdote is the same as that told of Anaxibius by Xenophon, *Hellenica*, IV.8.32-39, but if so, the name is out of alphabetical order, and the mistake must be ancient.

154 See the note on *Moralia*, 190B, *supra*.

155 *Ibid.* (1).

156 *Ibid.* (2).

4. When it came to pass that he fell in trying to win independence for the Greeks who were living in the region of Thrace, the committee which was sent to Sparta waited upon his mother Argileonis. Her first question was whether Brasidas had come to his end honourably; and when the Thracians spoke of him in the highest terms, and said that there was no other like him, she said, "You have no knowledge of that, sirs, being from abroad; for Brasidas was indeed a good man, but Sparta has many better than he was."[157]

DAMONIDAS

Damonidas, being assigned to the last place in the chorus by the director, exclaimed, "Good! You have discovered, sir, how this place which is without honour may be made a place of honour."[158]

DAMIS

Damis, with reference to the instructions sent from Alexander that they should pass a formal vote deifying him, said, "We concede to Alexander that, if he so wishes, he may be called a god."[159]

DAMINDAS

When Philip invaded the Peloponnesus, and someone said, "There is danger that the Spartans may meet a dire fate if they do not make terms with the invader," Damindas exclaimed, "You poor womanish thing! What dire fate could be ours if we have no fear of death?"

157 See the note on *Moralia*, 190B (3), *supra*.

158 See the note on *Moralia*, 191F, *supra*.

159 *Cf.* Aelian, *Varia Historia*, II.19.

DERCYLIDAS

Dercylidas, when Pyrrhus had his army near Sparta,[160] was sent to him as ambassador; and when Pyrrhus stated that they must receive their king Cleonymus, or they would find out that they were no braver than any of the rest, Dercylidas interrupted to say, "If this man is a god, we do not fear him, for we are guilty of no wrong; but if he is a man, he is surely not superior to us."

DEMARATUS[161]

1. Demaratus, when Orontes had talked to him rather haughtily and someone remarked, "Orontes has treated you haughtily, Demaratus," said, "He has committed no fault against me; for it is those who talk to please that do harm, not those who talk with hatred at heart."

2. When someone asked why they visited disgrace upon those among them who lost their shields, but did not do the same thing to those who lost their helmets or their breastplates, he said, "Because these they put on for their own sake, but the shield for the common good of the whole line."

3. As he was listening to a musician, he said, "He seems to do his silly task fairly well."[162]

4. In a council meeting he was asked whether it was due to foolishness or lack of words that he said nothing. "But a fool," said he, "would not be able to

160 In 272 B.C..

161 King of Sparta *circa* 510 until 491 B.C., when he was deposed and went to Persia. In 490 B.C. he accompanied Xerxes in his invasion of Greece.

162 *Cf.* the similar remarks in *Moralia,* 220F (6) and 234D (42), *infra.*

hold his tongue."[163]

5. When someone inquired why he was an exile from Sparta, being a king, he said, "Because her laws are more powerful than I am."

6. When one of the Persians, by unremitting bribery, had got away from him his beloved youth, and said to him, "Ho, Spartan, I have captivated your beloved," he said, "Not you, I swear, but you have bought and paid for him!"

7. When one of the Persians deserted from the king and was persuaded by Demaratus to change his mind and return, and the king was going to have him put to death, Demaratus said: "For shame, your Majesty! To think that when this man was your enemy you could not punish him for his desertion but now that he has become your friend, you would put him to death!"

8. In answer to a man who was a parasite of the king and often jeered at him over his exile, he said, "I have no quarrel with you, my friend; for I have squandered my position in life."

Ecprepes

Ecprepes, an Ephor, cut out with an adze two of the nine strings of Phrynis the musician, saying, "Do not murder music."[164]

Epaenetus

Epaenetus said that liars are to blame for all sins and crimes.

---

163 *Cf.* the similar remark of Bias in *Moralia*, 503F, and of Solon in Stobaeus, *Florilegium*, xxxiv.15.

164 The story is repeated in Plutarch's *Life of Agis*, chap. x (799F), and with variations in *Moralia*, 84A, 238C (*infra*); Athenaeus 636E; Boethius, *De Musica*, i.1.

EUBOEDAS

Euboedas, on hearing some men praising the wife of another man, could not stomach it, saying, "In regard to a woman's endowments there should be absolutely no talk among those outside the family."[165]

EUDAMIDAS, SON OF ARCHIDAMUS[166]

1. Eudamidas, the son of Archidamus and the brother of Agis, seeing Xenocrates in the Academy, already well on in years, discussing philosophy with his acquaintances, inquired who the old man was. Somebody said that he was a wise man and one of the seekers after virtue. "And when will he use it," said Eudamidas, "if he is only now seeking for it?"[167]

2. Hearing a philosopher discoursing to the effect that the wise man is the only good general, he said, "The speech is admirable, but the speaker is not to be trusted; for he has never been amid the blare of trumpets."[168]

3. Xenocrates had been expounding his theme, and had just reached the stopping-point when Eudamidas arrived. One of the persons with him remarked, "Just when we arrive he comes to the stopping-point." "Quite properly so," said Eudamidas, "if he has already said all he wanted to say." "It would have been nice to hear him," said the oth-

165 *Cf.* the note on *Moralia*, 217F, *supra*.

166 Eudamidas I, king of Sparta, 330-300 (?) B.C..

167 *Cf.* the note on *Moralia*, 192A, *supra*.

168 Ibid.

er. "Indeed," said Eudamidas, "and if we came to a man who had just dined, should we insist that he eat another dinner?"

4. Someone inquired why, when the citizens professed to be all for war against the Macedonians, he himself decided in favour of keeping the peace. He replied, "Because I do not need to prove that they are lying."

5. When another man brought up their brave successes against the Persians, and was urgent for the war, Eudamidas said, "You do not seem to realize that your proposition is the same as fighting fifty wolves after overcoming a thousand sheep!"

6. When a certain musician made a great hit, they asked Eudamidas what he thought of the man, and he replied, "He has great power to charm in a trifling matter."

7. When someone praised Athens, he said "And who could praise that city deservedly, towards which nobody has ever felt any affection for having been made a better man by it?"

8. When a man from Argos said that the Spartans became more unscrupulous on going abroad and being out of the control of their long-established laws,[169] he said, "But you, when you come to Sparta, do not become worse, but better."

9. When Alexander caused proclamation to be made at Olympia that all exiles might return to their own land,[170] save only the Thebans, Eudamidas said, "The proclamation for you, men of Thebes, is unfortunate, but very complimentary; for it is you only that Alexander fears."

10. Being asked for what purpose they offered

---

169 "Lions at home, but foxes abroad" was proverbial. *Cf.* Plutarch's *Comparison of Lysander and Sulla*, chap. iii (476E).

170 In 323 B.C. *Cf.* Diodorus, XVIII.8.

sacrifice to the Muses before hazardous ventures, he said, "So that our deeds may find good words."[171]

EURYCRATIDAS, SON OF ANAXANDRIDAS[172]

Eurycratidas, the son of Anaxandridas, when someone inquired why the Ephors try cases involving contracts[173] each day, said "So that also amid our enemies we may trust one another."

ZEUXIDAMUS[174]

1. When someone inquired why they kept the laws in regard to bravery unwritten, and did not have them written down and thus give them to the young men to read, Zeuxidamus said, "Because the young ought to accustom themselves to deeds of manly valour, a better thing than to apply their mind to writings."

2. When a certain Aetolian asserted that, for those who are able to play the part of real men, war is better than peace, Zeuxidamus said, "By Heaven, no; but for such men death is better than life."

HERONDAS

Herondas was at Athens when a man there was found guilty on a charge of not having any occu-

---

171 *Cf. Moralia*, 238B, *infra*; Plutarch's *Life of Lycurgus*, chap. xxi (53D).

172 Presumably Eurycratidas, son of Anaxander, mentioned by Herodotus, VII.204, in the genealogy of Leonidas. He was king of Sparta in the first half of the sixth century B.C..

173 *Cf.* Aristotle, *Politics*, III.1.10 (1275B).

174 Presumably the son of Leotychidas II, king of Sparta (*Moralia*, 224E). He died before his father, and so never became king.

pation,[175] and when he heard of this, he bade them point out to him the man who had been convicted of the freeman's crime![176]

THEARIDAS

Thearidas, as he was whetting his sword, was asked if it was sharp, and he replied, "Sharper than slander."

THEMISTEAS

Themisteas foretold to Leonidas, the king, the coming destruction both of himself and of his fellow-soldiers at Thermopylae, for he was a prophet. He was sent away by Leonidas to Sparta, on the pretext of announcing there what would come to pass, but in reality so that he should not suffer death with the rest. He, however, would not brook this, but said, "I was sent out to fight, not to carry messages."[177]

THEOPOMPUS[178]

1. Theopompus, in answer to a man who asked how anyone could keep a kingdom most securely, said, "If he concede to his friends their just share of frank speech, and, so far as lies in his power, do not suffer any of his subjects to be wronged."

---

175 On the subject see Busolt, *Griechische Staatskunde* (Munich, 1926), p815.

176 *Cf.* Plutarch's *Life of Lycurgus*, chap. xxiv (54E). The free population of Sparta did no labour.

177 A somewhat different version is to be found in *Moralia*, 866C. The original is in Herodotus, VII.221, where the seer's name is given as Megistias.

178 King of Sparta at the time of the first Messenian war, eighth (?) century B.C..

2. In answer to a man from abroad who said that among his own citizens he was called a lover of Sparta, he said, "It would be better to be called a lover of your own country than a lover of Sparta."

3. When the ambassador from Elis said that his citizens had sent him for the especial reason that he alone emulated the Spartan way of living, Theopompus said, "Is your way of living or that of the other citizens better?" And when the man said that his own was, Theopompus said, "How, then, can that State be saved in which, among many citizens, only one is a good man?"

4. When someone said that Sparta was saved through its kings, because they were competent to rule, he said, "Not so, but through its citizens, because they are obedient to the rulers."[179]

5. When the people of Pylos voted him some unusually high honours, he wrote in reply that time increases modest honours, but obliterates those that are extravagant.

6. When someone pointed out to him a wall, and inquired if it was strong and high, he said, "Is it not a place where women live?"[180]

THORYCION

Thorycion, arriving from Delphi and seeing in the Isthmus the forces of Philip, who had already gained possession of the narrow entrance, said, "The Peloponnesus has poor gate-keepers in you, men of Corinth!"

179 *Cf. Moralia*, 816E, and Plutarch's *Life of Lycurgus*, chap. xxx (58D).

180 *Cf.* the note on 190A, *supra*. This paragraph is not found in some MSS..

Thectamenes

Thectamenes, when the Ephors condemned him to death, went away smiling. Someone among the bystanders asked him if he felt such contempt for the laws of Sparta. "No," said he, "but I rejoice to think that I must pay this penalty myself without begging or borrowing anything from anybody."[181]

Hippodamus[182]

Hippodamus, when Agis was taking his place on the field of battle beside Archidamus, was sent with Agis to Sparta to render his services there. "But look you," said he, "I shall meet no more honourable death than in playing the part of a brave man for Sparta's sake." (He was over eighty years old.) And thereupon, seizing his arms and taking his stand at the king's right hand, he fell fighting.

Hippocratidas[183]

1. This is the answer of Hippocratidas to the governor of Caria who wrote a letter to him because a man from Sparta had been privy to the plot of certain conspirators, and had said nothing about it; and the governor added a line, asking how he should deal with him. Hippocratidas wrote

181 *Cf.* Cicero, *Tusculan Disputations*, i.42 (100).

182 The attempt has been made to identify Hippodamus with the Hippodamus mentioned in Athenaeus, 452a and in Polyaenus, *Strategemata*, ii.15, and, by emendation, to reconcile this passage with the time of Agis IV; but both Agis II and Agis III had fathers named Archidamus, and it is quite possible that the incident of sending away from danger the old man and the young heir to the throne took place as here narrated.

183 The name occurs in Herodotus, viii.131, as one of the earlier kings of Sparta.

in reply: "If you have done him any great favour, put him to death; but if not, expel him from your country, for he is a poltroon so far as any virtue is concerned."

2. When a youth with a lover in attendance met him one day, and turned colour, he said, "You ought to walk with persons such that when you are seen with them you shall keep the same complexion."

CALLICRATIDAS[184]

1. Callicratidas, an admiral, when Lysander's friends made him a fair offer that he permit them to make away with one of their enemies and receive ten thousand pounds, although he was in sore need of money for rations for his sailors, would not consent. Cleander, who was a member of his council, said, "But I would take it, if I were you." "And so would I," said Callicratidas, "if I were you!"[185]

2. When he came to Cyrus the Younger at Sardis (who was allied with the Spartans) to get money for his fleet, on the first day he bade them send in word that he wished to have an audience with Cyrus. But when he was told that Cyrus was busy drinking, he said, "I will wait till he has finished drinking." And at that time he withdrew, when he realized that it was not possible to meet Cyrus on that day, thus creating the impression that he was somewhat lacking in manners. On the succeeding day, when he was again told that Cyrus was drinking and would not come forth, he said, "We must not be so eager to get money as to do anything unworthy of Sparta," and withdrew to Ephesus, invoking many

184 Upright and straightforward Spartan who commanded the Spartan fleet at the battle of Arginusae in 406 B.C. He was killed in the battle.

185 *Cf.* the reply of Alexander, *Moralia*, 180c (11).

evil curses on those who were first wantonly treated by the barbarians and had taught the barbarians to be arrogant because of wealth. And he swore to the persons present that, just so soon as he should arrive at Sparta, he would do everything to bring about a reconciliation among the Greeks, that they might become more formidable to the barbarians, and cease begging them for their resources to use against one another.[186]

3. Being asked what kind of men the Ionians were, he said, "Poor freemen, but good slaves."[187]

4. When Cyrus sent on money to pay the soldiers, and special presents for himself as a token of friendship, he took the money only and sent back the presents, saying that there was no need of any private friendship between him and Cyrus, but the general friendship which had been contracted with all the Spartans would also serve for him.[188]

5. As he was about to engage in the naval battle at Arginusae, Hermon the pilot said that it would be well to sail away, for the ships of the Athenians were many more in number; but Callicratidas said, "And what of that? To flee is a disgrace and an injury to Sparta. No; to stay here, be it death or be it victory, is best."[189]

6. As he offered sacrifice before the battle, and heard from the seer that the indications of the omens were victory for the army, but death for its commander, he said, not at all disconcerted, "Sparta's fate rests not with one man. For, if I am killed,

---

186 *Cf.* Plutarch's *Life of Lysander*, chap. vi (436c); Xenophon, *Hellenica*, I.6.6-7.

187 *Cf.* the note on *Moralia*, 190F (1), *supra.*

188 *Cf. Moralia*, 213D (69), *supra.*

189 *Cf.* Xenophon, *Hellenica*, I.6.32; Cicero, *De officiis*, I.24 (84).

my country will not be impaired in any way; but if I yield to the enemy, it will be."[190] And so, after appointing Cleander to take his place as commander, he put forth without delay for the naval engagement, and met his death in the battle.

CLEOMBROTUS, SON OF PAUSANIAS[191]

Cleombrotus, the son of Pausanias, when a man from abroad was disputing with Cleombrotus's father about excellence, said, "My father is a better man than you — until you too have become a father."[192]

CLEOMENES, SON OF ANAXANDRIDAS[193]

1. Cleomenes, the son of Anaxandridas, said that Homer was the poet of the Spartans, and Hesiod of the Helots; for Homer had given the necessary directions for fighting, and Hesiod for farming.[194]

2. Having made an armistice of seven days with the Argives, he kept a watch on them, and on the third night, when they were sleeping because of their reliance on the truce, he attacked them, and slew some and took the others prisoners.[195]

---

190 *Cf.* Plutarch's *Life of Pelopidas*, chap. ii (177D).

191 King of Sparta, 380-371 B.C..

192 *Cf. Moralia*, 227F (14), *infra*, and Plutarch's *Life of Lycurgus*, chap. xv (48C).

193 King of Sparta, *circa* 517-488 B.C..

194 *Cf.* Aelian, *Varia Historia*, XIII.19.

195 *Cf.* Cicero, *De officiis*, I.10 (33). Herodotus, VI.78-79 (followed by other writers), relates that Cleomenes defeated the Argives by a

3. When he was reproached for his violation of the oath, he said that he had not included the nights as well as the days in his plighted word; and anyway, whatever ill one can do to one's enemies is regarded, among both gods and men, as something vastly higher than justice.[196]

4. It was his fortune to be repulsed from Argos, to gain which he had violated the truce, owing to the women's taking down the weapons in the shrines and defending themselves against him with these.[197] Later he went out of his mind, and, getting hold of a small dagger, he slashed himself, beginning with his ankles until he reached the vital parts, and thus departed this life laughing and grinning.[198]

5. The seer tried to dissuade him from leading his army against the city of the Argives, for the return, he said, would be made in disgrace. But when Cleomenes had advanced near the city, and saw the gates closed and the women upon the walls, he said, "Does it seem to you that the return from here can be made in disgrace, where, since the men are dead, the women have barred the gates?"

6. In answer to those of the Argives who upbraided him as an impious perjurer, he said, "You have the power to speak ill of me, but I have the power to do ill to you."

7. To the ambassadors from Samos who urged him to make war upon the despot Polycrates, and

---

different trick.

196 For the phrase *cf.* Euripides, *Electra*, 584; and Nauck, *Trag. Graec. Frag.*, Euripides, no. 758. .

197 *Cf. Moralia*, 245D, *infra;* Pausanias, II.20.8; Polyaenus, VIII.33.

198 *Cf.* Herodotus, VI.75 and 84; Athenaeus, 427C; Aelian, *Varia Historia*, II.41. His madness was traditionally ascribed to over-indulgence in strong drink.

for this reason spoke at great length, he said, "What you said at the beginning I do not remember; for that reason I do not comprehend the middle part; and the conclusion I do not approve."[199]

8. A certain pirate overran the country, and, when he was captured, said, "I had not the means to provide subsistence for my soldiers; therefore, to those who had it, but would not willingly give it, I came with the purpose of taking it by force." To this Cleomenes said, "Villainy is curt."

9. When a certain low fellow spoke ill of him, he said, "So it is for this reason, is it, that you speak ill of everyone, that we, busied in defending ourselves, may not have time to speak of your baseness?"

10. When one of the citizens said that the good king ought to be mild at all times and in every way, he remarked, "Yes, but not to the extent of being despised."

11. When he was afflicted with a lingering illness, and began to give attention to mind-healers and seers, to whom formerly he had given no attention, someone expressed surprise. "Why are you surprised?" said he; "for I am not now the same man that I was, and, not being the same man, I do not approve the same things."[200]

12. When a public lecturer spoke at considerable length about bravery, he burst out laughing and when the man said, "Why do you laugh, Cleomenes, at hearing a man speak about bravery, and that, too, when you are a king?" "Because, my friend," he said, "if it had been a swallow speaking

199 *Cf.* Herodotus, III.46, and the note on 216A (15), *supra*. The traditional date of the mission from Samos (525 B.C.) seems too early to fall within Cleomenes's reign, but the chronology is uncertain.

200 For a similar change in the attitude of Pericles and of Bion *cf.* Plutarch's *Life of Pericles*, chap. xxxviii (173A) and Diogenes Laertius, IV.54.

about it, I should have done the same thing, but if it had been an eagle, I should have kept very quiet."

13. When the people of Argos asserted that they would wipe out their former defeat[201] by fighting again, he said, "I wonder if by the addition of a word of two syllables[202] you have now become more powerful than you were before!"

14. When someone upbraided him, saying, "You are inclined to luxury, Cleomenes," he said, "Well, that is better than being unjust. And you are avaricious though you possess property enough."

15. When someone, wishing to introduce a musician to him, said, in addition to other commendations, that the man was the best musician among the Greeks, Cleomenes pointed to one of the persons near, and said, "Yonder man, I swear, ranks with me as the best soup-maker."[203]

16. Maeandrius, the despot of Samos, because of the inroad of the Persians, fled to Sparta, and exhibited all the gold and silver vessels which he had brought with him, and offered to favour Cleomenes with as many as he wished; but he would have none, and taking good care that the man should not distribute any among the rest of the citizens, he went to the Ephors and said that it was better for Sparta that his own friend and guest from Samos should withdraw from the Peloponnesus, so that he should not persuade anyone of the Spartans to become a bad man. And they listened to his advice and proclaimed the expulsion of Maeandrius that

201 Presumably in the battle over Thyrea in 546 B.C. *Cf.* Herodotus, I.82, and the reference in Plato, *Phaedo*, 89c.

202 The word "again." They had lost in the previous fighting.

203 *Cf. Moralia*, 218c (3) *supra*, where the saying is attributed to Archidamus II.

very day.[204]

17. When someone said, "Why have you not killed off the people of Argos who wage war against you so often?" he said, "Oh, we would not kill them off, for we want to have some trainers for our young men."

18. When somebody inquired of him why Spartans do not dedicate to the gods the spoils from their enemies, he said, "Because they are taken from cowards."[205]

Cleomenes, son of Cleombrotus

Cleomenes, the son of Cleombrotus, when someone offered him fighting cocks and said that they would die fighting for victory, said, "Well then, give me some of those that kill them, for those are better than these."[206]

Labotas[207]

Labotas, when someone spoke at very great length, said, "Why, pray, such a big introduction to a small subject? For proportionate to the topic should be the words you use."[208]

---

204 The story is taken from Herodotus, III.148, in part word for word.

205 *Cf. Moralia*, 224F (4) *infra*.

206 *Cf.* the note on *Moralia*, 191F, *supra*.

207 An early king of Sparta.

208 *Cf.* the note on *Moralia*, 208C (3), *supra*.

LEOTYCHIDAS[209]

1. Leotychidas the First, when somebody remarked to him that he was very changeable, said, "Yes, because of varying occasion; not like all you because of your baseness."

2. In answer to the man who asked how any man could best preserve his present state of good fortune, he said, "By not trusting everything to chance."

3. Being asked what freeborn boys had best learn, he said, "Those things which may help them when they become men."[210]

4. When someone inquired for what reason the Spartans drank so little, he said "So that others may not deliberate over us, but we over others."

LEOTYCHIDAS, SON OF ARISTON[211]

1. Leotychidas, the son of Ariston, in answer to a man who said that the sons of Demaratus were speaking ill of him, remarked, "Egad, I don't wonder; for not one of them could ever speak a good word."[212]

2. When at the adjacent gate a snake had coiled around the key, and the soothsayers declared this to be a prodigy, he said, "It doesn't seem so to me, but if the key had coiled around the snake, that

209 King of Sparta in the seventh century B.C..

210 *Cf.* the note on *Moralia*, 213D (67), *supra*.

211 Doubtless the son of Menares, Leotychidas II, king of Sparta, *circa* 491-469 B.C..

212 The same story is found in Diogenes Laertius, II.35 (of Socrates), and in Stobaeus, *Florilegium*, XIX.5 (of Plato).

would be a prodigy!"[213]

3. This is his retort to Philip, the priest of the Orphic mysteries, who was in the direst straits of poverty, but used to assert that those who were initiated under his rites were happy after the conclusion of this life; to him Leotychidas said, "You idiot! Why then don't you die as speedily as possible so that you may with that cease from bewailing your unhappiness and poverty?"[214]

4. When someone inquired why they did not dedicate to the gods the arms taken from the enemy, he said that property wrested from its owners owing to cowardice it is not good either for the young men to see, or to dedicate to the gods.[215]

LEO, SON OF EURYCRATIDAS[216]

1. When Leo, the son of Eurycratidas, was asked what kind of a city one could live in so as to live most safely, he said, "Where the inhabitants shall possess neither too much nor too little, and where right shall be strong and wrong shall be weak."

2. Seeing that the runners at Olympia were eager to gain some advantage in starting, he said, "How much more eager are the runners for a quick start than for fair play!"

3. When someone, at an inappropriate time, discoursed about some matters which were not unprofitable, he said, "My friend, in needless time

---

213 The saying is attributed to the others also; *cf.* Clement of Alexandria, *Stromata*, VIII.843 ed. Potter; or III.18, ed. Stahlin; Cicero, *De divinatione*, II.28 (62).

214 *Cf.* Diogenes Laertius, VI.4, where the remark is attributed to Antisthenes.

215 *Cf. Moralia*, 224B (18), *supra*.

216 King of Sparta in the first half of the seventh century B.C..

you dwell upon the need!"[217]

Leonidas, son of Anaxandridas[218]

1. Leonidas, the son of Anaxandridas and the brother of Cleomenes, in answer to a man who remarked, "Except for your being king, you are no different from the rest of us," said, "But if I were no better than you others, I should not be king."

2. His wife Gorgo inquired, at the time when he was setting forth to Thermopylae to fight the Persian, if he had any instructions to give her, and he said, "To marry good men and bear good children."[219]

3. When the Ephors said that he was taking but few men to Thermopylae, he said, "Too many for the enterprise on which we going."[220]

4. And when again they said, "Hae ye decided to dae aught else save to keep the barbarians from gettin' by?" "Nominally that," he said, "but actually expecting to die for the Greeks."

5. When he had arrived at Thermopylae he said to his comrades in arms, "They say that the barbarian has come near and is comin' on while we are wastin' time. Truth, soon we shall either kill the barbarians, or else we are bound to be killed oursel's."

6. When someone said, "Because of the arrows

217 *Cf.* the note on *Moralia*, 216F (2), *supra*.

218 The hero of Thermopylae. These sayings were doubtless incorporated, or meant to be incorporated, in Plutarch's *Life of Leonidas*, according to what he says in *Moralia*, 866B; and some of them may be found in *Moralia*, 854E-874D (*De Herodoti malignitate*).

219 *Cf. Moralia*, 240E (6), *infra*, and 866B.

220 *Ibid. Cf.* also 225B (8 and 9), *infra*, and 866B.

of the barbarians it is impossible to see the sun," he said, "Won't it be nice, then, if we shall have shade in which to fight them?"[221]

7. When someone else said, "They are near to us," he said, "Then we also are near to them."[222]

8. When someone said, "Leonidas, are you here to take such a hazardous risk with so few men against so many?" he said, "If you men think that I rely on numbers, then all Greece is not sufficient, for it is but a small fraction of their numbers; but if on men's valour, then this number will do."

9. When another man remarked the same thing he said, "In truth I am taking many if they are all to be slain."[223]

10. Xerxes wrote to him, "It is possible for you, by not fighting against God but by ranging yourself on my side, to be the sole ruler of Greece." But he wrote in reply, "If you had any knowledge of the noble things of life, you would refrain from coveting others' possessions; but for me to die for Greece is better than to be the sole ruler over the people of my race."

11. When Xerxes wrote again, "Hand over your arms," he wrote in reply, "Come and take them."

12. He wished to engage the enemy at once, but the other commanders, in answer to his proposal, said that he must wait for the rest of the allies. "Why," said he, "are not all present who intend to fight?[224] Or do you not realize that the only men

---

221 The remark is attributed to Dieneces by Herodotus, VII.226. *Cf.* Stobaeus, *Florilegium*, VII.46; Valerius Maximus, III.7, ext. 8; Cicero, *Tusculan Disputations*, I.42 (101).

222 *Cf. Moralia*, 194D, *supra*, and 234B.

223 *Cf. Moralia*, 225A (3), *supra*, and 866B.

224 *Cf. Moralia*, 185F, *supra*.

who fight against the enemy are those who respect and revere their kings?"

13. He bade his soldiers eat their breakfast as if they were to eat their dinner in the other world.[225]

14. Being asked why the best of men prefer a glorious death to an inglorious life, he said, "Because they believe the one to be Nature's gift but the other to be within their own control."

15. Wishing to save the lives of the young men, and knowing full well that they would not submit to such treatment, he gave to each of them a secret dispatch,[226] and sent them to the Ephors. He conceived the desire to save also three of the grown men, but they fathomed his design, and would not submit to accepting the dispatches.[227] One of them said, "I came with the army, not to carry messages, but to fight;" and the second, "I should be a better man if I stayed here"; and the third, "I will not be behind these, but first in the fight."

Lochagus

Lochagus, the father of Polyaenides and Seiron, when word was brought to him that one of his sons was dead, said, "I have known this long while that he was fated to die."

---

225 *Cf.* Cicero, *Tusculan Disputations*, i.42 (101); Valerius Maximus, iii.2, ext. 3.

226 The reference is to a well-known form of cipher message in use among the Spartans. A narrow leather thong was wrapped around a cylinder, and on the surface thus formed the message was written. When the thong was received it was applied to a duplicate cylinder kept by the recipient, and so the message was read.

227 *Cf. Moralia*, 866b; and Herodotus, vii.221, 229, 230.

LYCURGUS[228]

1. Lycurgus, the lawgiver, wishing to recall the citizens from the mode of living then existent, and to lead them to a more sober and temperate order of life, and to render them good and honourable men (for they were living a soft life), reared two puppies of the same litter; and one he accustomed to dainty food, and allowed it to stay in the house; the other he took afield and trained in hunting. Later he brought them into the public assembly and put down some bones and dainty food and let loose a hare. Each of the dogs made for that to which it was accustomed, and, when the one of them had overpowered the hare, he said, "You see, fellow-citizens, that these dogs belong to the same stock, but by virtue of the discipline to which they have been subjected they have turned out utterly different from each other, and you also see that training is more effective than nature for good."[229]

But some say that he did not bring in dogs which were of the same stock, but that one was of the breed of house dogs and the other of hunting dogs; then he trained the one of inferior stock for hunting, and the one of better stock he accustomed to dainty food. And afterwards, as each made for that to which it had become accustomed, he made it clear how much instruction contributes for better or worse, saying, "So also in our case, fellow-citizens, noble birth, so admired of the multitude, and our being descended from Heracles does not bestow any advantage, unless we do the sort of things for which he was manifestly the most glorious and

228 The reputed founder of the Spartan constitution. A brief account of his laws may be found also in Porphyry, *De abstinentia*, IV.3 ff. .

229 As in *Moralia*, 3A.

most noble of all mankind, and unless we practise and learn what is good our whole life long."

2. He made a redistribution of the land, and assigned an equal share to all the citizens; and it is said that a while later, on returning from abroad, as he passed through the country, where the harvesting had just been finished, and saw the cocks of grain standing near together in even lines, he was much pleased, and said with a smile to those who were with him that it looked as if all the Spartan land belonged to many brothers who had recently divided it.[230]

3. Having introduced the abolition of debts, he next undertook to divide equally all household furnishings, so as to do away completely with all inequality and disparity. But when he saw that the people were likely to demur about assenting to this outright spoliation, he decreed that gold and silver coin should in future have no value, and ordained that the people should use iron money only. He also limited the time within which it was lawful to exchange their present holdings for this money. When this had been done, all wrongdoing was banished from Sparta. For nobody was able to steal or to accept a bribe or to defraud or rob any more, when the result was something of which concealment was not possible, nor was its acquisition envied, nor its use without risk, nor its exportation or importation safe. As an added measure, he brought about the banishment from Sparta of everything not absolutely necessary. And, by reason of this, no merchant, no public lecturer, no soothsayer or mendicant priest, no maker of fancy articles ever made his way into Sparta. The reason was that he

230 Related with more detail by Plutarch in his *Life of Lycurgus*, chap. vii (44A).

permitted no handy coinage to circulate among them, but instituted the iron coinage exclusively, which in weight was over a pound and a quarter, and in value not quite a penny.[231]

4. Having determined to make an attack upon the prevailing luxury, and to do away with the rivalry for riches, he instituted the common meals. And in answer to those who sought to know why he had established these, and had divided the citizens, when under arms, into small companies, he said, "So that they may get their orders promptly, and, in case they cherish any radical designs, the offence may be confined to a small number; also that there may be for all an equal portion of food and drink, and so that not only in drink or food, but in bedding or furniture or anything else whatsoever, the rich man may have no advantage at all over the poor man."[232]

5. Having made wealth unenviable, since nobody could make any use or show of it, he said to his intimate friends, "What a good thing it is, my friends, to show in actual practice the true characteristic of wealth, that it is blind!"[233]

6. He took good care that none should be allowed to dine at home and then come to the common meal stuffed with other kinds of food and drink. The rest of the company used to berate the man who did not drink or eat with them, because they felt that he was lacking in self-control, and was

231 Plutarch tells all this, at somewhat greater length, in his *Life of Lycurgus*, chap. ix (44D). *Cf.* also Xenophon, *Constitution of Sparta*, 7.5 and 6; Plato, *Eryxias*, 400B; Pollux, *Onomasticon*, VII.105, and IX.79; Justin, *Historiae Philippicae*, III.2.11-12.

232 Plutarch amplifies this account in his *Life of Lycurgus*, chap. x (45B).

233 *Ibid.* (45C).

too soft for the common way of living.[234] Moreover, a fine was laid upon the man who was detected. A case in point is that of Agis, their king, who, returning from a long campaigning in which he had overcome the Athenians in war, wished to dine at home with his wife on this one day, and sent for his allowance of food; but the military commanders would not send it; and the following day, when the matter was disclosed to the Ephors, he was fined by them.[235]

7. The well-to-do citizens resented legislation of this type, and, banding together, they denounced him and pelted him, wishing to stone him to death. As he was being pursued, he rushed through the market-place; and he out-distanced almost all his pursuers, and gained refuge in the shrine of Athena of the Brazen House; only, as he turned around, Alcander, who was pursuing him, put out one of his eyes by a stroke of his staff. But when, later, Lycurgus received Alcander, who was handed over to him for punishment by vote of the people, he did not treat him ill nor blame him, but, by compelling him to live under the same roof with him, he brought it to pass that Alcander had only commendation for Lycurgus and for the manner of living which he had found there, and was altogether enamoured of this discipline. Lycurgus dedicated a memorial of his unhappy experience in the shrine of Athena of the Brazen House, and gave to her the added epithet of Optilletis; for the Dorians in this part or world call the eyes 'optics (*optilloi*).'[236]

---

234 *Ibid.* (45D).

235 *Cf.* Plutarch's *Life of Lycurgus*, chap. xii (46C).

236 Plutarch tells the story more fully in his *Life of Lycurgus*, chap. xi (45D-46A); *cf.* also Aelian, *Varia Historia*, XIII.23, and Stobaeus, *Florilegium*, XIX.13.

8. Being asked why he had not made any use of written laws, he said, "Because those who are trained and disciplined in the proper discipline can determine what will best serve the occasion."[237]

9. At another time when some sought to know why he had ordained that the people should use only an axe in putting a roof on their houses, and make a door with a saw only and none of the other tools, he said, "So that the citizens may be moderate in regard to all the things which they bring into the house, and may possess none of the things which are the cause of rivalry among other peoples."[238]

10. It was because of this custom also that their first king Leotychidas, dining at somebody's house[239] and observing the construction of the ceiling, which was expensive and embellished with panels, asked his host if timbers grew square in their country!

11. Being asked why he had prohibited frequent campaigns against the same foes, he said, "So that they may not, by becoming accustomed to defending themselves frequently, become skilled in war." It was for this reason also that there appeared to be no slight ground for complaint against Agesilaus, who by his almost continual inroads and campaigns into Boeotia had rendered the Thebans a match for the Spartans. At any rate Antalcidas, when he saw him wounded, exclaimed, "You have got a handsome reward as you deserve for your fostering care in teaching them to give when they did not wish to

237 *Cf.* Plutarch's *Life of Lycurgus*, chap. xiii (47A).

238 *Cf.* Plutarch's *Life of Lycurgus*, chap. xiii (47C), and *Moralia*, 189E (3), *supra*.

239 In Corinth, according to Plutarch's *Life of Lycurgus*, chap. xiii (47C); *cf.* also *Moralia*, 189E, *supra*, and the note.

fight and did not even know how."[240]

12. When someone else desired to know why he instituted strenuous exercise for the bodies of the maidens in races and wrestling and throwing the discus and javelin, he said, "So that the implanted stock of their offspring, by getting a strong start in strong bodies, may attain a noble growth, and that they themselves may with vigour abide the birth of their children and readily and nobly resist the pains of travail; and moreover, if the need arise, that they may be able to fight for themselves, their children, and their country."[241]

13. When some persons expressed disapproval of the nudity of the maidens in the processions, and sought to know the reason for it, he said, "So that they, by following the same practices as the men, may not be inferior to them either in bodily strength and health or in mental aspirations and qualities, and that they may despise the opinion of the crowd." Wherefore is recorded also in regard to Gorgo, the wife of Leonidas, a saying to this effect: when some woman, a foreigner presumably, remarked to her, "You Spartan women are the only women that lord it over your men," she replied, "Yes, for we are the only women that are mothers of men!"[242]

14. By excluding the unmarried from looking on at the festival of the naked youth, and by laying upon them other additional disgrace, he created much concern about having children. He also

240 *Cf.* Plutarch's *Life of Lycurgus*, chap. xiii (47D), and *Moralia*, 189D, *supra*, and the note.

241 *Cf.* Plutarch's *Life of Lycurgus*, chap. xiv (47F); Suidas, *Lexicon*, under Lycurgus.

242 *Cf. Moralia*, 240E (5) *infra*, and Plutarch's *Life of Lycurgus*, chap. xiv (47E-48B).

deprived them of the honour and attention which the young bestowed on their elders. And nobody said a word against the remark which was made to Dercylidas, although he was a general and in high repute; for one of the younger men, as Dercylidas approached, did not rise to offer his seat, saying, "No, for you are not the father of any son who will rise and offer his seat to me."[243]

15. When someone inquired why he had made a law that girls should be given in marriage without any dowry, he said, "So that some of them shall not be left unwedded because of lack of means, and some shall not be eagerly sought because of abundant wealth, but that each man, with an eye to the ways of the maid, shall make virtue the basis of his choice." For this reason he also banished from the State all artificial enhancement of beauty.[244]

16. He set limits to the time of marriage for both men and women, and, in answer to the man who inquired about this, he said, "So that the offspring may be sturdy by being sprung from mature parents."[245]

17. In answer to a man who expressed surprise because he debarred the husband from spending the nights with his wife, but ordained that he should be with his comrades most of the day and pass the whole night in their company, and visit his bride secretly and with great circumspection, he said, "So that they may be strong of body and never become sated, and that they may be ever fresh in affection, and that the children which they bring into

243 *Ibid.* chap. xv (48c); and *Moralia,* 223A, *supra.*

244 *Cf.* Aelian, *Varia Historia,* VI.6.

245 *Cf.* Plutarch's *Life of Lycurgus,* chap. xv (48D), and Xenophon, *Constitution of Sparta,* 1.6.

the world may be more sturdy."[246]

18. He banished perfume on the ground that it spoiled and ruined the olive oil,[247] and also the dyer's art on the ground that it was a flattery of the senses.

19. To all whose business was the enhancement of personal beauty he made Sparta forbidden ground, for the reason that they outraged the arts through the vileness of their art.[248]

20. So strict in those times was the virtue of the women, and so far removed from the laxity of morals which later affected them,[249] that in the earlier days the idea of adultery among them was an incredible thing. There is still recalled a saying of a certain Geradatas, a Spartan of the very early times, who, on being asked by a foreigner what was done to adulterers in their country, since he saw that there had been no legislation by Lycurgus on that subject, said, "Sir, there is never an adulterer in our country." But when the other retorted with, "Yes, but if there should be?" Geradatas said, "His penalty is to provide an enormous bull which by stretching his neck over Mount Taygetus can drink from the river Eurotas." And when the other in amazement said, "But how could there ever be a bull of that size?" Geradatas laughed and said, "But how could there ever be an adulterer in Sparta, in which wealth and luxury and adventitious aids to beauty are held in disesteem, and respect and good order

246 *Cf.* Plutarch's *Life of Lycurgus*, chap. xv (48E), and Xenophon, *Constitution of Sparta*, 1.5.

247 *Cf.* Seneca, *Quaestiones Naturales*, IV.13.9. Perfumes in ancient times were made with a base of oil; *cf. Moralia*, 127B.

248 *Cf.* Plutarch's *Life of Lycurgus*, chap. ix (p. 44F).

249 Athenaeus, 142F, quotes Phylarchus at some length regarding the degeneration of the Spartans.

and obedience to authority are given the highest place?"[250]

21. In answer to the man who was insistent that he establish a democracy in the State Lycurgus said, "Do you first establish a democracy in your own house."[251]

22. When someone inquired why he ordained such small and inexpensive sacrifices to the gods, he said, "So that we may honour the Divine powers without ceasing."[252]

23. As he permitted the citizens to engaged only in that kind of athletic contests in which the arm is not held up,[253] somebody inquired what was the reason. He replied, "So that no one of the citizens shall get the habit of crying quits in the midst of a hard struggle."[254]

24. When someone asked why he ordered a frequent change of camping-place, he said, "So that we may inflict greater injury upon our enemies."[255]

25. When someone sought to know why he forbade assaults on walled places, he said, "So that valiant men may not suffer death at the hands of a

---

250 In part this is in close agreement with Plutarch's *Life of Lycurgus*, chap. xv (49c), but the main point, which is lacking in the MSS., is usually inserted here by the editors from the *Life*.Critical note to the Greek:ταῦρον ἐκτίνει μέγαν . . . τηλικοῦτος; *γελάσας*] Xylander from the *Life of Lycurgus*, chap. xv: MSS. have only ταῦτον ἔφη ὁ Γεραδάτας.

251 *Cf.* the note on *Moralia,* 189E (2), *supra.*

252 *Cf.* the note on *Moralia* 172B, *supra.*

253 As a sign of defeat; *cf.* E. Norman Gardiner, *Greek Athletic Sports and Festivals* (London, 1910), p415.

254 *Cf.* the note on 189E (4), *supra.*

255 *Cf.* Xenophon, *Constitution of Sparta,* 12.5.

woman or a child or some such person."[256]

26. When some of the Thebans advised with him in regard to the sacrifice and the lamentation which they perform in honour of Leucothea, he advised them that if they regarded her as a goddess they should not bewail her, but if they looked upon her as a woman they should not offer sacrifice to her as to a goddess.[257]

27. In answer to some of the citizens who desired to know, "How we can keep off any invasion by enemies," he said, "If you remain poor, and no one of you desires to be more important than another."[258]

28. And at another time, when they raised a question about fortifications, he said that a city is not unfortified whose crowning glory is men and not bricks and stones.[259]

29. The Spartans gave particular attention to their hair, recalling a saying of Lycurgus in reference to it, that it made the handsome more comely and the ugly more frightful.[260]

30. He gave instructions that in war, when they had put the enemy to flight and had gained a victory, they should continue the pursuit only far enough to make their success assured, and then return immediately; for he said that it was neither a noble

256 *Cf.* Plutarch's *Comparison of Lysander and Sulla,* 477D. As a matter of fact, the Spartans were quite without ability to attack a walled town, as is clear from Herodotus, IX.70, and Thucydides, Thucydides, I.102.

257 This saying of Xenophanes seems to have been attributed by someone to Lycurgus. *Cf. Moralia,* 171E, 379B, and 763C; also Aristotle, *Rhetoric,* II.23.27.

258 *Cf.* Plutarch's *Life of Lycurgus,* chap. xix (52B).

259 *Cf.* the note on *Moralia,* 210E (29), *supra.*

260 *Cf.* the note on *Moralia,* 189E (1), *supra.*

trait nor a Greek trait to slay those who had yielded, and this policy was not only honourable and magnanimous, but useful as well; for the opposing army, knowing that they customarily spared those who surrendered, but made away with those who resisted, would regard it as more profitable to flee than to stay.[261]

31. When somebody inquired why he forbade spoiling the enemy's dead, he said, "So that the soldiers may not, by looking about covertly for spoil, neglect their fighting, but also that they may keep to their poverty as well as to their post."[262]

LYSANDER

1. When Dionysius, the despot of Sicily, sent costly garments for Lysander's daughters, he would not accept them, saying that he was afraid that because of them his daughters would appear ugly rather than beautiful.[263] But a little later, when he was sent as ambassador to the same despot from the same State, Dionysius sent to him two robes and bade him choose whichever one of them he would, and take it to his daughter; but Lysander said that she herself would make a better choice, and, taking them both, he departed.

2. Lysander, who was a clever quibbler, and given to employing cunning deceptions to further most of his designs, counted justice as mere expediency, and honour as that which is advantageous. He said that the truth is better than falsehood, but that the worth and value of either is determined by

---

261 *Cf.* Plutarch's *Life of Lycurgus*, chap. xxi (54A); Thucydides, v.73; Polyaenus, *Strategemata*, I.16.3.

262 *Cf. Moralia*, 224B (16), *supra*.

263 *Cf.* the note on *Moralia*, 190E (1), *supra*.

the use to which it is put.[264]

3. In answer to those who blamed him because his carrying out most of his designs through deception, which they said was unworthy of Heracles,[265] and gaining his successes by wile in no straightforward way, he said laughing that where he could not get on with the lion's skin it must be pieced out with the skin of the fox.[266]

4. When others censured him for his violation of his oaths which he had made in Miletus he said that one must trick children with knuckle-bones, but men with oaths.[267]

5. He conquered the Athenians by a ruse at Aegospotami, and by pressing them hard through famine he forced them to surrender their city, whereupon he wrote to the Ephors, "Athens is taken."[268]

6. In answer to the Argives, who were disputing with the Spartans in regard to the boundaries of their land and said that they had the better of the case, he drew his sword and said, "He who is master of this talks best about boundaries of land."[269]

7. Seeing that the Boeotians were wavering at

---

264 *Cf.* Plutarch's *Life of Lysander*, chap. vii (437A).

265 The legendary ancestor of both lines of Spartan kings; *cf.* Herodotus, VII.204 and VIII.131.

266 *Cf.* the note on *Moralia*, 190E (2), *supra*.

267 Repeated in *Moralia*, 330F, where it is attributed to Dionysius; *Moralia*, 741C; Diodorus, x.9.1; Dio Chrysostom, *Oration* LXXIV (399 R., 640 M.); Polyaenus, *Strategemata*, I.45.3; and Aelian, *Varia Historia*, VII.12, who says that some attribute it to Lysander, and others to Philip of Macedon.

268 According to Plutarch, *Life of Lysander*, chap. xiv (441B), the Ephors objected to the verbosity of the dispatch!.

269 *Cf.* the note on *Moralia*, 190E (3), *supra*.

the time when he was about to pass through their country he sent to them to inquire whether he should march through their land with spears at rest or ready for action.[270]

8. When a Megarian in the common council used plain words to him, he said, "My friend, your words need a city to back them."[271]

9. When the Corinthians had revolted and he was going through their country along by the walls and saw that the Spartans were reluctant to attack, a hare was seen leaping across a ditch, whereupon he said, "Are you not ashamed, men of Sparta, to be afraid of such enemies as these, who are so slack that hares sleep in the walls of their city?"[272]

10. As he was consulting the oracle in Samothrace, the priest bade him tell what was the most lawless deed that had ever been committed by him in his lifetime. Lysander asked, "Must I do this at your command or at the command of the gods?" When the priest said, "At the command of the gods," Lysander said, "Then do you take yourself out of my way, and I will tell them in case they inquire."[273]

11. When a Persian asked what kind of government he commended most highly, he said, "The government which duly awards what is fitting to both the brave and the cowardly."

12. In answer to a man who said that he commended him and was very fond of him, he said "I have two oxen in a field, and although they both may utter no sound, I know perfectly well which one is lazy and which one is the worker."

---

270 *Cf.* Plutarch's *Life of Lysander*, chap. xxii (445D).

271 *Cf.* the note on *Moralia*, 190F (5), *supra*.

272 *Cf.* the note on *Moralia*, 190E (4), *supra*.

273 *Cf.* the note on *Moralia*, 217C (1), *supra*.

13. When someone was reviling him, he said, "Talk right on, you miserable foreigner, talk, and don't leave out anything if thus you may be able to empty your soul of the vicious notions with which you seem to be filled."

14. Some time after his death, when a dispute arose regarding a certain alliance, Agesilaus came to Lysander's house to examine the documents in regard to this, for Lysander had kept these at his own house. Agesilaus found also a book written by Lysander in regard to the government, to this effect: that the citizens should take away the kingship from the Eurypontids and the Agiads[274] and put it up for election, and make their choice from the best men, so that this high honour should belong not to those who were descended from Heracles, but to men like Heracles, who should be selected for their excellence; for it was because of such excellence that Heracles was exalted to divine honours. This document Agesilaus was bent upon publishing to the citizens, and demonstrating what kind of a citizen Lysander had been in secret, and with the purpose also of discrediting the friends of Lysander. But they say that Cratidas, who at that time was at the head of the Ephors, anxious lest, if the speech should be read, it might convert the people to this way of thinking, restrained Agesilaus and said that he ought not to disinter Lysander, but to inter the speech along with him, since it was composed with a vicious purpose and in a plausible vein.[275]

15. The suitors of his daughters, when after his death he was found to be a poor man, renounced their obligations; but the Ephors punished them because when they thought he was rich they courted

274 *Cf.* the note on *Moralia*, 231c (1), *infra*.

275 *Cf.* the note on *Moralia*, 212c (52), *supra*.

his favour, but when they found from his poverty that he was just and honest they disdained him.[276]

NAMERTES

Namertes was sent as an ambassador, and when one of the people in that country congratulated him because he had many friends, he asked if this man had any sure means of testing the man of many friends; and when the other desired to learn, Namertes said, "By means of misfortune."[277]

NICANDER[278]

1. Nicander, when someone said that the Argives were speaking ill of him, said, "Well then, they are paying the penalty for speaking ill of the good!"[279]

2. When someone inquired why the Spartans wore their hair long and cultivated beards, he said, "Because for a man his own adornment is the very beside and cheapest."[280]

3. When one of the Athenians said, "Nicander, you Spartans insist too much on your principle of doing no work," he said, "Quite true; we do not make work of this thing or that thing in your hap-

276 *Cf.* Plutarch's *Life of Lysander*, chap. xxx (451A), and Aelian, *Varia Historia*, vi.4, and x.15.

277 *Cf.* John Heywood, *Proverbs*, part i chap. 11: "but indeede a friend is never known till a man have neede.".

278 An early Spartan king, perhaps *circa* 809-770 B.C. He was the son of Charillus (*Moralia*, 189F, *supra*).

279 He was invading Argolis and laying waste the country; see Pausanias, iii.7.4.

280 *Cf.* the note on *Moralia*, 189F (3), *supra*.

hazard fashion."[281]

PANTHOEDAS[282]

1. Panthoedas went on embassy to Asia and when they pointed out to him a very strong wall he said, "By Heaven, strangers, fine quarters for women!"[283]

2. When the philosophers in the Academy were conversing long and seriously, and afterwards some people asked Panthoidas how their conversation impressed him, he said, "What else than serious? But there is no good in it unless you put it to use."[284]

PAUSANIAS,[285] THE SON OF CLEOMBROTUS

1. Pausanias, son of Cleombrotus, at the time when the people of Delos were asserting their rightful claims to the island against the Athenians, and said that according to the law[286] which prevailed among them there were no births and no burials in the island, said, "How can this be your native land in which no one of you has ever been born nor shall ever be hereafter?"[287]

---

281 *Cf. Moralia,* 348F and 710F; Plato, *Laws,* 803C-D. See also the note on *Moralia,* 221C, *supra.*

282 A Spartan harmost who fell at Tanagra, 377 B.C..

283 *Cf.* the note on *Moralia,* 190A, *supra.*

284 *Cf. Moralia,* 192B, 220D, and 1033B-E.

285 Regent of Sparta from 479 B.C.; commander at Plataea.

286 The law seems to have been put into effect (426-425 B.C.) some years after the death of this Pausanias (468 B.C.).

287 *Cf.* Thucydides, III.104.

2. When the exiles were inciting him to lead his army against the Athenians, and saying that, when his name was proclaimed at Olympia, they were the only people who hissed him, he said, "What do you think that those who hissed when they were being well treated will do if they are treated ill?"[288]

3. When someone inquired why the Spartans had made Tyrtaeus the poet a citizen, he said, "So a stranger shall never appear as our leader."[289]

4. In answer to the man who was weak in body, but was urging that they risk a battle against the enemy by both land and sea, he said, "Are you willing to strip yourself and show what kind of man you are — you who advise us to fight?"

5. When some people were amazed at the costliness of the raiment found among the spoils of the barbarians, he said that it would have been better for them to be themselves men of worth than to possess things of worth.[290]

6. After the victory at Plataea over the Persians he ordered that the dinner which had been prepared for the Persians should be served to himself and his officers. As this had a wondrous sumptuousness, he said, "By Heaven, the Persian was a greedy fellow who, when he had all this, came after our barley-cake."[291]

---

288 A similar remark is attributed to Philip of Macedon in *Moralia*, 143F, 179A, and 457F.

289 Tyrtaeus, according to tradition, was a native of Athens.

290 *Cf.* Plato, *Laws*, 870B; Cicero, *Paradoxa Stoicorum*, VI.1-3 (42-52).

291 *Cf.* Herodotus, IX.82.

Pausanias, the son of Pleistoanax[292]

1. Pausanias, the son of Pleistoanax, in answer to the question why it was not permitted to change any of the ancient laws in their country, said, "Because the laws ought to have authority over the men, and not the men over the laws."

2. When, in Tegea, after he had been exiled,[293] he commended the Spartans, someone said, "Why did you not stay in Sparta instead of going into exile?" And he said, "Because physicians, too, are wont to spend their time, not among the healthy, but where the sick are."[294]

3. When someone inquired of him how they could become able to conquer the Thracians, he said, "If we should make the best man our general."

4. When a physician paid him a visit and said, "You have nothing wrong with you," he said, "No, for I do not employ you as my physician."

5. When one of his friends blamed him because he spoke ill of a certain physician, although he had never had anything to do with him, and had not suffered any harm at his hands, he said, "Because if I had ever had anything to do with him I should not now be alive."

6. When the physician said to him, "You have lived to be an old man," he said, "That is because I never employed you as my physician."

7. He said that the best physician was the man who did not allow his patients to rot, but buried them quickly.

292 King of Sparta, 408-394 B.C..

293 In 394 B.C..

294 *Cf.* the similar saying which is attributed to Aristippus in Diogenes Laertius, II.70.

PAEDARETUS[295]

1. Paedaretus, when someone said that the enemy were many in number, remarked, "Then we shall be the more famous, for we shall kill more men."

2. Seeing a certain man who was effeminate by nature, but was commended by the citizens for his moderation, he said, "People should not praise men who are like to women nor women who are like to men, unless some necessity overtake the woman."

3. When he was not chosen as one of the three hundred,[296] which was rated as the highest honour in the State, he went away cheerful and smiling; but when the Ephors called him back, and asked why he was laughing, he said, "Because I congratulate the State for having three hundred citizens better than myself."[297]

PLEISTARCHUS[298]

1. Pleistarchus the son of Leonidas, in answer to one who asked him for what reason they did not take their titles from the names of the first kings, said, "Because the first kings needed to be absolute monarchs, but those who followed them had no such need."[299]

---

295 See the note on *Moralia*, 191F, *supra*.

296 *Cf.* Herodotus, VIII.124; Xenophon, *Constitution of Sparta*, 4.3.

297 *Cf.* the note on *Moralia*, 191F, *supra*.

298 King of Sparta, 480-458 B.C..

299 One of the two lines of the kings of Sparta was called "Agids" (or "Agiads") from Agis, the second of that line, and the other "Eurypontids" from Eurypon, the third of that line. *Cf.* Plutarch's *Life of Lycurgus*, chap. ii (40D); Strabo, VIII.366; Pausanias, III.7.1.Presumably Plutarch means that the later Spartan kings did not wish

2. When a certain advocate kept making jests, he said, "You had better be on your guard, my friend, against jesting all the time, lest you become a jest yourself, just as those who wrestle all the time become wrestlers."

3. In retort to the man who imitated a nightingale, he said, "My friend, I have had more pleasure in hearing the nightingale itself."[300]

4. When someone said that a certain evil-speaker was commending him, he said, "I wonder whether possibly someone may not have told him that I was dead; for the man can never say a good word of anybody who is alive."[301]

Pleistoanax[302]

Pleistoanax, the son of Pausanias, when an Attic orator called the Spartans unlearned, said, "You are quite right, for we alone of the Greeks have learned no evil from you."[303]

Polydorus[304]

1. Polydorus, the son of Alcamenes, when a certain man was continually making threats against his enemies, said, "Don't you see that you are using up the best part of your vengeance?"

2. As he was leading out his army to Messene,

---

to perpetuate the memory of any harshness, which would have been suggested by the names of the earlier absolute monarchs.

300 *Cf.* the note on *Moralia*, 212F (58), *supra*.

301 *Cf.* the note on *Moralia*, 224D (1), *supra*.

302 King of Sparta, 458-408 B.C..

303 *Cf.* the note on *Moralia*, 192B (1), *supra*.

304 King of Sparta in the second part of the eighth century B.C..

someone asked him if he was going to fight against his brothers. He said that he was not, but was merely proceeding to the unassigned portion of the land.

3. The Argives, after the battle of the three hundred,[305] were again overcome, with all their forces, in a set battle, and the allies urged Polydorus not to let slip the opportunity, but to make a descent upon the enemy's wall and capture their city; for this, they said, would be very easy, since the men had been destroyed and the women only were left. He said in answer to them, "To my mind it is not honourable, when fighting on even terms, to conquer our opponents, but, after having fought to settle the boundaries of the country, to desire to capture the city I do not regard as just; for I came to recapture territory and not to capture a city."

4. Being asked why the Spartans risked their lives so bravely in war, he said, "Because they have learned to respect their commanders and not to fear them."[306]

POLYCRATIDAS

Polycratidas was sent, along with others, as ambassador to the king's generals, and when these asked whether they were there as private citizens or had been sent as public representatives, he said, "If we succeed, public; if not, private."[307]

PHOEBIDAS[308]

Phoebidas, before the hazardous engagement at

305 Herodotus, I.82.

306 *Cf. Moralia,* 217A (5), and 227D (12).

307 *Cf.* Plutarch's *Life of Lycurgus,* chap. xxv (55C).

308 Spartan general, fourth century B.C..

Leuctra, when some remarked that this day would show the brave man, said that the day was worth much if it had the power to show the brave man.

SOÜS[309]

The story is told that Soüs being besieged by the Cleitorians in a rugged and waterless stronghold, agreed to give up to them the land which he had captured by the spear if all the men with him should drink from the neighbouring spring. This spring the enemy were guarding. When the oaths had been exchanged, he got together his men and offered the kingdom to the man who would not drink; however no one had the strength to resist, but they all drank; whereupon he came down after all the rest, and sprinkled himself, the enemy still being present, and went back and took possession of the land on the ground that he had not drunk.[310]

TELECLUS[311]

1. Teleclus, in answer to the man who said that Teleclus's father was speaking ill of him, said, "If he had had no cause to speak, he would not have spoken."

2. When his brother said to him that the citizens did not comport themselves toward himself as they did toward the king (although he was of the same family), but with much less consideration, he said, "The reason is, you do not know how to submit to

309 Third king of Sparta, second of the Eurypontid line according to tradition.

310 *Cf.* Plutarch's *Life of Lycurgus*, chap. ii (40c).

311 See the note on *Moralia*, 190A.

injustice, and I do."[312]

3. Being asked why it was the custom among them for the younger men to rise up and give place to the elder, he said, "So that, having this attitude regarding honour toward those who are not related to them, they may pay greater honour to their parents."[313]

4. When someone inquired how much property he possessed, he said, "Not more than enough."

CHARILLUS[314]

1. Charillus, being asked why Lycurgus made so few laws, said, "Because those who use few words have need of but few laws."[315]

2. When someone inquired why they took their girls into public places unveiled, but their married women veiled, he said, "Because the girls have to find husbands, and the married women have to keep to those who have them!"

3. When one of the Helots conducted himself rather boldly toward him, he said, "If I were not angry, I would kill you."[316]

4. When someone asked him what he thought to be the best form of government, he said, "That in which the greatest number of citizens are willing, without civil strife, to vie with one another in virtue."[317]

---

312 *Cf. Moralia,* 190A, *supra.*

313 *Cf. Moralia,* 237D, *infra;* Xenophon, *Constitution of Sparta,* 6.1-3.

314 An early king of Sparta; traditionally a contemporary of Lycurgus. Another spelling is CHARILAUS.

315 *Cf. Moralia,* 189F (1), *supra.*

316 *Cf. Moralia,* 189F (2), *supra.*

317 *Cf. Moralia,* 154E.

5. When someone inquired why all the statues of the gods erected among them were equipped with weapons,[318] he said, "So that we may not put upon the gods the reproaches which are spoken against men because of their cowardice, and so that the young men may not pray to the gods unarmed."

6. In answer to the man who inquired why they wore their hair long, he said, "Because this is the natural and inexpensive form of ornament."[319]

VARIOUS SAYINGS OF SPARTANS TO FAME UNKNOWN

1. When the ambassadors of the Samians spoke at great length, the Spartans said to them, "We hae forgot the first part, and the later part we did na ken because we hae forgot the first."[320]

2. When a speaker extended his remarks to a great length, and then asked for answers to report to his citizens, they said, "Report that you found it hard to stop speaking and we to listen."[321]

3. In answer to the Thebans who were disputing with them over some matters, they said, "You should have less pride or more power."[322]

4. A Spartan, being asked why he wore his beard so very long, said, "So that I may see my grey hairs and do nothing unworthy of them."

5. Another, in answer to the inquiry, "Why do you use short swords?" said, "So that we may get close to the enemy."

---

318 *Cf.*, for example, Head, *Historia Numorum* (Oxford, 1911), p434.

319 *Cf.* the note on *Moralia*, 189F (3), *supra*. .

320 *Cf. Moralia*, 216A (15), *supra*.

321 *Cf. Moralia*, 215E (9), *supra*.

322 *Cf. Moralia*, 218E (8), *supra*.

6. When someone was praising the Argive warriors, a Spartan said, "Yes, at Troy!"[323]

7. Another, being told that some people after dining are forced to drink,[324] said, "What, and are they forced to eat also?"

8. When Pindar wrote,[325] "Athens the mainstay of Greece," a Spartan said that Greece was like to fall if it rested on any such mainstay as that!

9. Someone on seeing a painting in which Spartans were depicted as slain by Athenians, kept repeating, "Brave, brave Athenians." A Spartan cut in with, "Yes, in the picture!"

10. To a man who was listening avidly to some spitefully slanderous remarks a Spartan said, "Stop being so generous with your ears against me!"[326]

11. To a man who was being punished, and kept saying, "I did wrong unwillingly," someone retorted, "Then take your punishment unwillingly."

12. Someone, seeing men seated on stools[327] in a privy, said, "God forbid that I should ever sit where it is not possible to rise and yield my place to an older man."[328]

13. When some Chians, on a visit to Sparta, vomited after dinner in the hall of the ephors, and

---

323 A thousand years before.

324 Perhaps the reference is to the expression πρὸς βίαν πίνειν found in Alcaeus (No. 20 in Bergk, *Poet. Lyr. Graec.* III p156), Sophocles (*Frag.* 669 Nauck) and Aristophanes (*Acharnians*, 73). *Cf.* also Menander, *The Arbitrants*, lines 4-5 (in *L. C. L.* p18) where the same words are used.

325 *Frag.* No. 76 (ed. Christ).

326 *Cf.* the similar remark of Simonides quoted in Stobaeus, *Florilegium*, II.42.

327 Not in Sparta, of course.

328 As in Plutarch's *Life of Lycurgus*, chap. xx (52F).

befouled with ordure the very chairs in which the Ephors were wont to sit, the Spartans, first of all, instituted a vigorous investigation, lest possibly these might be citizens; but when they learned that they were, in fact, Chians, they caused public proclamation to be made that 'The Spartans grant permission to the Chians to be filthy.'[329]

14. When someone saw almonds of the hard sort[330] selling at double the price of others, he said, "Are stones so scarce?"

15. A man plucked a nightingale and finding almost no meat, said, "It's all voice ye are, and nought else."[331]

16. One of the Spartans saw Diogenes the Cynic holding his arms around a bronze statue in very cold weather,[332] and asked Diogenes if he were cold, and when Diogenes said "No," the other said, "What great thing are you doing then?"

17. One of the people of Metapontum, being reproached for cowardice by a Spartan,[333] said, "But as a matter of fact we have not a little of the country of other states"; whereupon the Spartan replied, "Then you are not only cowardly, but also unjust."

18. A man who was visiting Sparta stood for a long time upon one foot, and said to a Spartan, "I do not think that you, sir, could stand upon one foot as long as that"; and the other interrupting said, "No,

---

329 A similar story is told of the Clazomenians by Aelian, *Varia Historia*, II.15.

330 *Cf.*, for example, Athenaeus, 53A.

331 Vox et praeterea nihil.

332 A part of his self-imposed training to inure himself to cold, as in the summer he used to roll in the hot sand to inure himself to heat, according to Diogenes Laertius, VI.23.

333 Possibly Cleonymus (Diodorus, XX.104).

but there is not a single goose that could not do it."

19. When a man boasted greatly of his art in speaking, a Spartan said, "By Heaven, there is no art nor can there be an art without a firm hold on truth."[334]

20. When an Argive said once upon a time, "There are many tombs of Spartans in our country," a Spartan said, "But there is not a single tomb of an Argive in our country," indicating by this that the Spartans had often set foot in Argos, but the Argives had never set foot in Sparta.[335]

21. A Spartan having been taken prisoner in war and put up for sale, when the crier said, "I offer a Spartan for sale," stopped his mouth, saying, "Cry a prisoner of war."[336]

22. One of the men serving in the army of Lysimachus, being asked by him whether he were not one of the Helots, said, "Do you suppose that any Spartan would come to get the sixpence which you pay?"

23. At the time when Thebans had conquered the Spartans at Leuctra and advanced to the river Eurotas itself, one of them, boasting, said, "Where are the Spartans now?" A Spartan who had been captured by them said, "They are not here; otherwise you would not have come thus far."

24. At the time when the Athenians had surrendered their city,[337] they declared it was only right that Samos should be left to them, but the Spartans said, "Do you, at a time when you do not even own

---

334 In almost the same words in Plato, *Phaedrus*, 260E.

335 *Cf.* Plutarch, *Life of Agesilaus*, chap. xxxi (613D).

336 *Cf. Moralia*, 234C (40), *infra.*

337 At the close of the Peloponnesian war, 404 B.C. Samos had been the naval base for the Athenians during the preceding years.

yourselves, seek to possess others?" From this incident arose the proverb:[338]

> Who does not own himself would Samos own.

25. When the Spartans had taken by storm a certain city, the Ephors said, "Gone is the wrestling-school of our young men; they no longer will have competitors."[339]

26. When their king promised to wipe out completely another city which, as it happened, had given much trouble to the Spartans, they would not allow it, saying, "You must not abolish nor remove the whetstone of our youth."

27. They appointed no trainers to instruct in wrestling so that the rivalry might not be in skill, but in courage.[340] This is the reason why Lysanoridas, when he was asked how Charon had conquered him, said, "By his great resourcefulness."

28. Philip wrote at the time when he entered their country, asking whether they wished that he should come as a friend or as a foe; and they made answer, "Neither."

29. They sent an ambassador to Antigonus, son of Demetrius, and, upon learning that the ambassador had addressed Antigonus as King, they fined him, although he had brought for each one of them a bushel and a half of wheat at a time when there was great scarcity of food.

30. When Demetrius complained that they had sent only one ambassador to him, they replied, "Is

---

338 *Cf.* Dio Chrysostom, *Oration* LXXIV (637 M., 395 R.); Leutsch and Schneidewin, *Paroemiographi Graeci*, I p292 (Diogenianus, VII.34), and II p571 (Aposto.

339 The last clause looks like an explanatory comment. Pantazides would omit it.

340 *Cf. Moralia*, 639F, and Plutarch's *Life of Pelopidas*, chap. vii (281B).

it not enough — one to one?"[341]

31. When a bad man brought in a very good idea, they accepted it; but they took it away from him and bestowed the right of proposing it upon another man who had lived a virtuous life.[342]

32. When two brothers quarrelled with each other, the Spartans fined the father because he permitted his sons to quarrel.

33. They fined a visiting harp-player because he played the harp with his fingers.[343]

34. The boys were fighting, and one of them wounded the other mortally with the stroke of a sickle. The friends of the wounded boy, as they were about to separate, promised to avenge him and make away with the one who had struck him, but the boy said, "In Heaven's name do not, for it is not right; the fact is, I should have done that myself if I had been quick enough and brave enough."

35. In the case of another boy, when the time had arrived during which it was the custom for the free boys to steal whatever they could, and it was a disgrace not to escape being found out, when the boys with him had stolen a young fox alive, and given it to him to keep, and those who had lost the fox came in search for it, the boy happened to have slipped the fox under his garment. The beast, however, became savage and ate through his side to the vitals; but the boy did not move or cry out, so as to avoid being exposed, and left, when they had departed, the boys saw what had happened,

341 *Cf. Moralia*, 216B (16), *supra*.

342 *Cf. Moralia*, 41B, and 801B; Aeschines, *Against Timarchus*, 180-181; Philo Judaeus, *The Worse Plotting against the Better*, 195B; Aulus Gellius, XVIII.

343 Thus making the music pleasanter to hear than if he had used the plectrum. *Cf. Moralia*, 802F.

and blamed him, saying that it would have been better to let the fox be seen than to hide it even unto death; but the boy said, "Not so, but better to die without yielding to the pain than through being detected because of weakness of spirit to gain a life to be lived in disgrace."[344]

36. Some people, encountering Spartans on the road, said, "You are in luck, for robbers have just left this place," but they said, "Egad, no, but it is they who are in luck for not encountering us."[345]

37. A Spartan being asked what he knew, said, "How to be free."

38. A Spartan boy, being taken captive by Antigonus the king and sold, was obedient in all else to the one who had bought him, that is, in everything which he thought fitting for a free person to do, but when his owner bade him bring him a chamber-pot, he would not brook such treatment, saying, "I will not be a slave"; and when the other was insistent, he went up to the roof, and saying, "You will gain much by your bargain," he threw himself down and ended his life.[346]

39. Another one being sold, when someone said, "If I buy you, will you be good and helpful?" said, "Yes, and if you do not buy me."[347]

40. Another captive being put up for sale, when the crier that he was offering a slave for sale, said, "You damnable wretch, won't you say 'a

344 The story is told more briefly in Plutarch's *Life of Lycurgus*, chap. xviii (51B).

345 *Cf.* the note on *Moralia*, 194D (3), *supra*.

346 *Cf. Moralia*, 242D (30), *infra*. This story is repeated by Philo Judaeus, *Every Virtuous Man is Free*, chap. xvii (882c); Seneca, *Epistulae Moral.* no. 77 (x.1.1.

347 *Cf. Moralia*, 242C (29), *infra*.

captive'?"[348]

41. A Spartan had as an emblem on his shield a fly, and that, too, no bigger than life-size. When some mockingly said that he had done this to escape being noticed, he said, "Rather that I may be noticeable; for I come so close to the enemy that my emblem is seen by them in its true size."

42. Another, when a lyre was brought in at an evening party, "It is not Spartan to indulge in nonsense."[349]

43. A Spartan, being asked if the road into Sparta were safe, said, "That depends on what kind of a mon ye are; for the lions gang about where they wull, but the hares we hunt over that land."

44. In a clinch one wrestler, who had the other by the neck, overpowered him with little effort, and pulled him to the ground. Since the one who was down was at a disadvantage in using his body, he bit the arm that held him. His opponent said, "Spartan, you bite like a woman." "No, indeed," said he, "but like a lion."[350]

45. A lame man was going forth to war, and some persons followed after him laughing. He turned around and said, "You vile noddles! A man does not need to run away when he fights the enemy, but to stay where he is and hold his ground."[351]

46. Another,[352] mortally wounded by an arrow,

---

348 *Cf. Moralia*, 233C (21), *supra*.

349 *Cf. Moralia*, 220A (3). For the expression of similar sentiments see Plutarch's *Life of Themistocles*, chap. ii (112c); Cicero, *Tusculan Disputations*, I.2 (4).

350 The same story is told of Alcibiades in *Moralia*, 186D (1), and in Plutarch's *Life of Alcibiades*, chap. i (192c).

351 *Cf. Moralia*, 210F (34), and 217C; Valerius Maximus, III.7, ext. 8.

352 Callicrates at the battle of Plataea (Herodotus, IX.72).

said, as his life was ebbing away, "I am not troubled because I must die, but because my death comes at the hands of a womanish archer, and before I have accomplished anything."[353]

47. A man stopped at an inn and gave the innkeeper a piece of meat to prepare; and when the innkeeper asked for cheese and oil besides, the other said, "If I had cheese, what need should I have of meat too?"[354]

48. In answer to the man who called Lampis[355] of Aegina happy, because he seemed very rich in having many cargoes on the sea in ships, a Spartan said, "I do not pay much attention to happiness that hangs by ropes!"[356]

49. When somebody told a Spartan that he was lying, the Spartan replied, "Yea, we are free men; but ithers, if they dinna tell the truth, will rue it."[357]

50. When someone set himself to make a corpse stand upright, and, for all his efforts, was unable to do this, he said, "Egad, there is need of something inside."

51. Tynnichus, when his son Thrasybulus was slain, bore it sturdily; and this epigram[358] was written on him:

---

353 Repeated by Plutarch, *Life of Aristeides*, chap. xvii (329c).

354 Repeated in *Moralia*, 995B, where the meat is fish. *Cf.* also Aelian, *Varia Historia*, 787A; Demosthenes, *Or.* xxiii.211 (691).

355 Lampis was famous for his ships and his wealth. *Cf.*, for example, *Moralia*, 787A; Demosthenes, *Or.* xxiii.211 (691).

356 *Cf.* Cicero, *Tusculan Disputations*, v.14 (40).

357 *Cf. Moralia*, 229A (2).

358 Attributed to Dioscorides in the *Palatine Anthology*, VII.229 (*The Greek Anthology* in the *L. C. L.*, II p130).

Lifeless to Pitane came, on his shield upborne, Thrasybulus;
Seven the wounds he received, pierced by the Argive spears;
All in the front did he show them; and him with his blood-stained body
Tynnichus placed on the pyre, saying these words in his eld:
"cowards be mourned, but with never a tear shall I bury
You, my son, who are mine, yea, and are Sparta's as well."

52. When the keeper of a bath was pouring in a great quantity of water for Alcibiades, a Spartan[359] said, "Why all this for him as if he were not clean? The fellow is pouring in extra water as if for a very dirty man."

53. When Philip of Macedon sent some orders to the Spartans by letter, they wrote in reply, "What you wrote about, 'No.'"[360] When he invaded the Spartans' country, and all thought that they should be destroyed, he said to one of the Spartans, "What shall you do now, men of Sparta?" And the other said, "What else than die like men? For we alone of all the Greeks have learned to be free, and not to be subject to others."[361]

54. After the defeat of Agis,[362] Antipater demanded fifty boys as hostages, but Eteocles, who was Ephor, said they would not give boys, lest the boys should turn out to be uneducated through missing the traditional discipline; and they would not be fitted for citizenship either. But the Spar-

359 The Spartans were not enthusiastic bathers (*cf. Moralia* 237B).

360 The story is told with slightly more detail in *Moralia*, 513A.

361 *Cf.* Cicero, *Tusculan Disputations*, v.14 (42).

362 Agis III, in 331 B.C..

tans would give, if he so desired, either old men or women to double the number. And when Antipater made dire threats if he should not get the boys, the Spartans made answer with one consent, "If the orders you lay upon us are harsher than death, we shall find it easier to die."[363]

55. While the games were being held at Olympia, an old man was desirous of seeing them, but could find no seat. As he went to place after place, he met with insults and jeers, and nobody made room for him. But when he came opposite the Spartans, all the boys and many of the men arose and yielded their places. Whereupon the assembled multitude of Greeks expressed their approbation of the custom by applause, and commended the action beyond measure; but old man, shaking his head grey-haired and grey-bearded,[364] and with tears in his eyes, said, "Alas for the evil days! Because all the Greeks know what is right and fair, but the Spartans alone practise it."

Some say that the same thing happened at Athens also. It was at the time of the Panathenaic festival, and the people of Attica were teasing an old man in an unseemly manner, calling him to them as if they were intending to make room for him, and not making room if he came to them. When he had passed through almost all the spectators and came opposite the delegates of the Spartans, they all arose from where they were sitting and gave him place. The crowd, delighted, applauded the action with great approval, and one of the Spartans said, "Egad, the Athenians know what is right and fair,

---

363 A different version of the Spartans' reply is given in *Moralia*, 64D.

364 Homer, *Il.* XXII.74, and XXIV.516. .

but do not do it."[365]

56. A beggar asked alms of a Spartan, who said, "If I should give to you, you will be the more a beggar; and for this unseemly conduct of yours he who first gave you is responsible, for he thus made you lazy."

57. A Spartan, seeing a man taking up a collection for the gods, said that he did not think much of gods who were poorer than himself.

58. A man who caught another in adultery with an ugly woman said, "Puir soul! what was yer muckle need?"[366]

59. Another, listening to an orator rolling off long sentences, said, "Egad, but the man has courage; he twists his tongue well about no subject at all."

60. One man who came to Sparta, and observed the honour which the young render to the old, said, "Only in Sparta does it pay to grow old."[367]

61. A Spartan, being asked what kind of a man Tyrtaeus the poet was, said, "A good man to sharpen the spirit of youth."

62. Another who had sore trouble with his eyes was going forth to war; and when some said to him, "Where are you going in that state, or what do you purpose to do?" he said, "Even if I accomplish nothing else, I may at least blunt an enemy's sword."

63. Bulis and Sperchis of Sparta went as volunteers to Xerxes king of the Persians, to render satisfaction which Sparta owed according to an oracle, because the people had killed the heralds sent to

---

365 *Cf.* Cicero, *De senectute*, 18 (63-64); Valerius Maximus, IV.5, ext. 2.

366 In *Moralia*, 525D, the same saying is attributed to a man of Byzantium.

367 A similar sentiment is attributed to Lysander by Cicero, *De senectute*, 18 (63).

them by the Persian. These men came before Xerxes and bade him make away with them in any manner he desired, as representing the Spartans. But when he, filled with admiration, let them go free, and was insistent that they remain with him, they said, "And how should we be able to live here, abandoning our country and laws and those men in whose behalf we made such a long journey to die?" And when Indarnes[368] the general besought them at greater length, and said that they would receive equal honour with the friends of the king who stood highest in advancement, they said, "You seem to us not to know what is the meed of liberty, which no man of sense would exchange for the kingdom of the Persians."[369]

64. Because a friend with whom a Spartan was intending to stay dodged him on the first day, and on the next day, having borrowed bedding, received him sumptuously, the Spartan jumped on the bedding and trod it under foot, remarking that it was because of this that yesterday he had not had even straw to sleep on.

65. Another, on going to Athens, saw that the Athenians were hawking salt fish and dainties, collecting taxes, keeping public brothels, and following other unseemly pursuits, and holding none of them to be shameful. When he returned to his own country, his fellow-citizens asked how things were in Athens, and he said, "Everything fair and lovely," speaking sarcastically and conveying the idea that among the Athenians everything is considered fair and lovely, and nothing shameful.

---

368 Hydarnes in Herodotus, vii.135.

369 *Cf. Moralia*, 815e; Dio Chrysostom, *Or.* lxxvi *ad fin.*; Stobaeus, *Florilegium*, vii.70, and xxxix.27 (quoting Serenus). The ultimate source.

66. Another, being asked a question, answered "No." And when the questioner said, "You lie," the other said, "You see, then, that it is silly of you to ask questions to which you know the answer!"

67. Once upon a time, ambassadors from Sparta arrived at the court of Lygdamis the despot. But as he tried to put them off and repeatedly postponed the interview, and, to crown all, it was asserted that he was in a delicate condition, the Spartans said, "Tell him, in God's name, that we have not come to wrestle with him, but to have a talk with him."

68. When someone, initiating a Spartan into the Mysteries, asked him what his conscience told him was the most unholy deed he had ever done, he said, "The gods know." And when the other became even more insistent, and said, "It is absolutely necessary that you tell," the Spartan asked in turn, "To whom must I tell it? To you or to the god?" And when the other said, "To the god," the Spartan said, "You go away then."[370]

69. Another, passing by a tomb at night, and imagining that he saw a ghost, ran at it with uplifted spear, and, as he thrust at it, he exclaimed, "Where are you fleeing from me, you soul that shall die twice?"

70. Another, having vowed to throw himself from the Leucadian cliff, went up and came down again after seeing the height. Being jeered at for this, he said, "I did na think my vow needed anither greater vow to dae it!"

71. Another, in the thick of the fight, was about to bring down his sword on an enemy when the recall sounded, and he checked the blow. When someone inquired why, when he had his enemy in

370 A similar story is told of Antalcidas, *Moralia*, 217C (1), and of Lysander, *Moralia*, 229D (10), *supra*.

his power, he did not kill him, he said, "Because it is better to obey one's commander than to slay an enemy."[371]

72. Someone said to a Spartan who was defeated at Olympia, "Spartan, your opponent proved himself the better man." "No," said he, "not that, but more upsetting!"[372]

371 *Cf. Moralia,* 273F; Plutarch's *Comparison of Pelopidas and Marcellus,* chap. iii (317D); Epictetus, II.6. The source is doubtless Xenophon, *Cyropaedia,* IV.1.3, and Chrysantas is the man's name.

372 For a similar sentiment see *Moralia,* 233E (27), *supra.*

www.ingramcontent.com/pod-product-compliance
Lightning Source LLC
Chambersburg PA
CBHW032020180726
48283CB00008B/2767
* 9 7 8 1 9 4 8 6 4 8 1 1 0 *